FESTIVAL in a BOOK

A Celebration of Wenlock Poetry Festival

Edited by Liz Lefroy

904 Press

First published in the UK in 2023 on behalf of Wenlock Poetry Festival
by 904 Press, 7b St Mary's Street, Shrewsbury, SY1 1EB, 904Press@gmail.com

Concept for the anthology copyright © Liz Lefroy, 2023

ISBN: 978-1-7393787-0-7

Cover and book design copyright © Gabriel Watt, 2023

Photographs copyright © Emily Wilkinson, 2023

Wenlock Poetry Festival gratefully acknowledges the financial support it received
from Arts Council England

Thanks to Raven Studios, Shrewsbury for the bursary supporting the design
input of Gabriel Watt

Printed and bound in Great Britain by Orphans Press Ltd, Leominster

FESTIVAL PROGRAMME

A Festival Toast

1. Carol Ann Duffy

Welcome to Festival in a Book

2. Anna Dreda

Opening Night at the Edge

5. Introduced by Lisa Blower

Liz Berry   Robin Robertson   Philip Gross   Jonathan Edwards
Andrew McMillan   Imtiaz Dharker
Daljit Nagra   Andrew Motion   Jean Sprackland   Paul Henry

Much Wenlock

21. Introduced by Paul Francis

Lucy Ingrams   Ross Donlon   Barry Tench   Ian Duhig
Jean Atkin   Ian Parr   Carol Caffrey

Festival Poetry Breakfast

33. Introduced by Anna Dreda

Kim Moore   Tess Jolly   Char March   Catherine Graham   Meg Cox
Brian Patten   Carole Bromley   Rory Waterman
John Foggin   David Constantine   Amanda Dalton   Kathryn Bevis

Workshop

Publisher in Residence
Nine Arches Press

Deborah Alma   Josh Ekroy   Abegail Morley   Julia Webb
Robert Peake   Jo Bell   Roy McFarlane
Gregory Leadbetter   Daniel Sluman   Isobel Dixon

Young Wenlock

Roger McGough   Roger Stevens   Emma Purshouse
Gareth Owen   Angela Topping   Chrissie Gittins
Andrew Fusek Peters   Shauna Darling Robertson   Morar Lucas

Young Wenlock Workshop

Priory Hall

Helen Mort   Alison Brackenbury   Clare Shaw   Adam Horovitz
Luke Wright   Mario Petrucci
Steve Griffiths   Stevie Ronnie   Menna Elfyn
Sean Borodale
Luke Kennard   Fiona Sampson

The Busk

Helen Kay   Hollie McNish   Paul Henry   Nadia Kingsley
Thirza Clout   Jen Hawkins   Ted Eames   Tor Cotton
Mary Cunningham   Steve Pottinger
Dairena Ní Chinnéide   Sally Crabtree   Martin Figura
LiTTLe MACHiNe   Martin Thomas   John Hegley

Workshop

Borderlands

Ian McMillan   Fred D'Aguiar   Anna Selby   Rosie Shepperd
Emily Wilkinson   Suzanne Iuppa   Gill McEvoy
Lucy Rose Cunningham   Chris Kinsey   David Whyte

Workshop

Behind the Scenes

Liz Lefroy   Frieda Hughes   R.V. Bailey   Paul Francis
Pat Edwards   Bethany Rivers
Carol Forrester   Beverley Fry   Roger Garfitt

Closing Night

Jackie Kay   Hannah Lowe   Katrina Naomi   Ann Gray
Pauline Prior-Pitt   Liz Lochhead
Pascale Petit   Gillian Clarke   Carol Ann Duffy

Vote of Thanks

The Afterparty

Helen Ivory   Steve Harrison   Will McCartney
Kate Innes

The Poetree

Catherine Benbow   Linda Richards   Ted Eames
Veronica Miller   David Bingham   Tor Cotton   Jonathan Day
Zadie Loft   Jeff Phelps   Robert Petty   Lorna Taylor
Jo Jackson   Mary Elliott   Michael W. Thomas
Marion Molteno   Melanie Revolta   Charlotte Rigarlsford
Pupils from Sound Primary School

Acknowledgements

Index of Poets & Poems

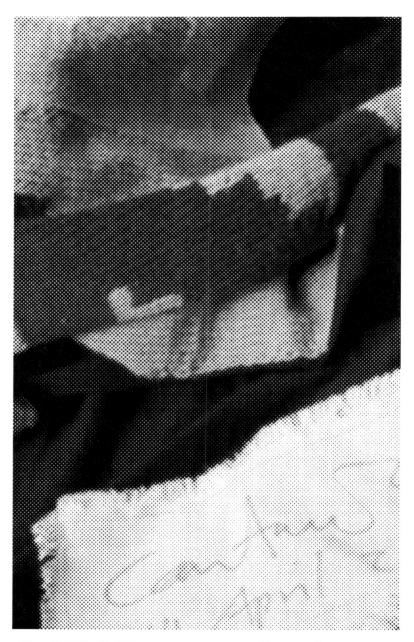

A FESTIVAL TOAST

What Anna Dreda achieved in creating and continuing the Wenlock Poetry Festival was a remarkable and inspirational act of love. The poetry world – poets, performers, readers, and audiences – needs its Saints, and Anna is a Poetry Saint. Building outwards from her jewel of a bookshop and into the small town she adored, she performed the miracle of a Poetry Festival which lives still in the pages of this book.

Anna will thank the poets, of course, but on behalf of the poets I thank her. So let us all raise our glass to Anna Dreda. Thank you, Anna, for all those days of community, language, passion, and laughter. You added to the world, and we love you.

Carol Ann Duffy

WELCOME TO FESTIVAL IN A BOOK

Wenlock Poetry Festival's inception happened in the best of ways – a conversation among friends round a kitchen table. It was my first time meeting Gillian Clarke, who was at that time the National Poet of Wales. She was the special guest at our annual Readers Retreat. Gillian and I sat next to each other at dinner and talked about books and poetry and bookshops. By the end of the conversation she promised me that her friend, Carol Ann Duffy, would love to come and visit my bookshop and to do a poetry event for us there.

Sure enough, Carol Ann got in touch (this was a few months before her acceptance of the Laureateship was announced) and duly came to Much Wenlock. A poetry reading was arranged at the Edge Arts Centre. I'm sure the 220 people there will always remember what a marvellous event it was. When I was taking Carol Ann to catch her train the next day, she said how much she had enjoyed the quality of attentiveness: the real, deep listening from the audience (something that poets would comment on time and again), and that we should start a Poetry Festival in Much Wenlock. Not one to miss an opportunity, I said I would start a Festival if she would be our founding patron; she agreed.

Having Carol Ann on board saved us several years of the hard slog of getting established. She gave me a list of some of her current favourite poets and permission to use her name when inviting them. What a sign of faith in us that was. Being able to write to poets saying, "Carol Ann Duffy has suggested I invite you…" was the best endorsement a brand new Festival could ever have had. I will always be grateful.

Carol Ann said that Much Wenlock was the perfect place for poetry, and it was. Our little town is pretty, and traditional, and tiny – full of coffee shops and independent shops of all kinds. It's fair to say that the town opened its arms very widely. And the sun always shone at Festival time – honestly!

The town, the volunteers, and the poets all worked incredibly hard to create Festival magic – a magic our audiences fondly recall, and which still hovers around the streets of Wenlock.

Welcome to the part of Wenlock Poetry Festival that continues in this *Festival in a Book*. Just like those spring weekends, it's full of new and well-loved poems, and of labels from the virtual Poetree contributed by a whole host of Festival-goers. The magic is abundantly evident in the pages of this beautiful, wonderful book that Liz Lefroy has created with the generosity of audiences, volunteers, and friends. And the poets, of course: some have become friends, some have gone on to become prize-winners. All are excellent poets who give unstintingly of themselves in their work. Their poetry enriches our lives. I thank them for it.

Anna Dreda

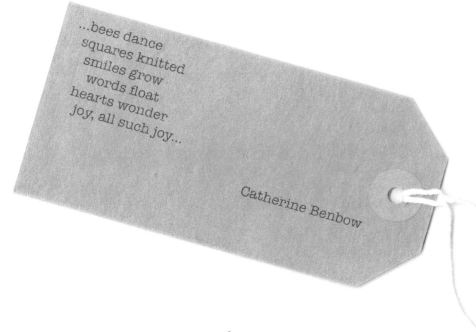

...bees dance
squares knitted
smiles grow
words float
hearts wonder
joy, all such joy...

Catherine Benbow

OPENING NIGHT AT THE EDGE

Opening Nights can be the most exciting of events and the most terrifying. In 2015, I remember being in a state of frazzled awe as Hannah Lowe took to the stage, knowing that her voice would launch a hundred others sharing thousands of words over a single weekend.

I almost didn't hear the poetry. The venue was packed. I was checking the lighting and the sound; could those at the back hear? Then my phone buzzed. A fellow poet had arrived early, and they'd come to hear Hannah, followed by Luke Kennard, and then Kei Miller who'd won the Forward Prize that year. I went to meet them and ushered them in as Hannah read her poems from *Chick*. I remember thinking, "It's all happening." The planning. The preparation. The promotion. It was all about the poetry now.

Lisa Blower

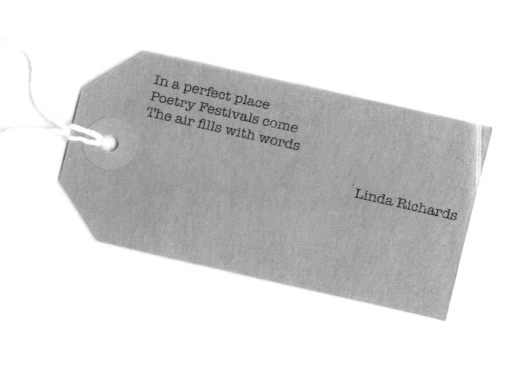

In a perfect place
Poetry Festivals come
The air fills with words

Linda Richards

LIZ BERRY

Blue Heaven

Our poem which art in blue heaven,
give us this morning,
daffodils spilling Spring's song like yolk,
moss sporing on the guttering, snug
for wet-the-beds; jenny-wren and weeping birch
watching over us, our unanswered emails
and half-built Lego palaces, milk cups
and toast crumbs, photographs of us
in the nineties, drunk and so in love
we look like children.
Give us griefs and small kindnesses,
wunce apon a time in clumsy boy's hand
on the back of a phone bill,
library books and Germolene, sanitary towels
soaked with clotted rubies,
pyjamas shed beneath the bunkbeds
like adder skins, money spiders, stories,
the nights we touch in darkness
with that wild honeymilk of recognition.
Tenderise our hearts to all that is holy:
the dog and her blanket, the playgroup collage,
and forgive us our trespasses –
pulling tight the shutters on our hearts
when others are knocking,
cussing in the night when we stumble to the cot.
Teach us to love each other as the tree loves the rain,
never wasting a drop.

Robin Robertson

Spring

Unlike the world that greens
around us, greens and dies
and greens again,
we only have a single turn at this:
one day's tide,
one year's worth of seasons;
we make these children – re-make
ourselves, our own beginnings –
because we only have
one spring, one flood,
one chance at life, at love,
before it closes over us, in the dark
on frozen shingle.

Philip Gross

A Modest Proposal

... and we'll build a house on the wind
whose almost weightless membranes flex
and ripple round us, like the flux
of light on water – a house of the mind

shared, minds together. So we'll rise
on our own thermal, fanned by sun-vanes
hushed as moth wings, as the trailing vines
of airstream dangle us, ripe fruit, and the rose

of the compass unpicking its petals – love
me, loves me not – at our feet, the known
world simmering with detail, vast and clear

without borders or ground-rent. We'll live
on the wind, in a sentence without nouns,
all verb: we'll be nowhere, everywhere and here.

Jonathan Edwards

Building my Grandfather

He comes flat-pack, a gift for my eighteenth.
We tip the bits out on the living room carpet:
nuts and bolts, a spanner, an Allen key,
tubes halfway between telescopes and weapons.
At first he goes together easily:
slippered left foot clicks into the ankle,
shin joins at a perfect right angle.
We have more of a problem with the right knee,
but my father remembers it was always gammy
from twelve-hour shifts, labouring in tight seams.
I fit the lungs, pumping in mustard gas
which filled each breath he took from 1918.
Something seems to be missing from the heart
and for a while we search beneath the sideboard,
but then my father says it's probably
for the old man's brother, who joined up when he did
and didn't make it back. The cheek and neck
and nose slot in and soon, we've almost got him:
my father holds the lips, the final bit
before he opens his eyes and I meet him.
A glance in the mirror at what he's going to see:
a pale-faced boy by an electric fire,
Nike swoosh like a medal on my chest.
It's then I say *Stop*. What will he make of me?

Andrew McMillan

boxing gloves

what else holds time like this? a face   a clock
the ground   the years of sweat that live inside
each fist   grip your hands for hours after

it's almost three-dimensional   the architecture
of the smell   its different musty rooms
in which each time each boy thrust out a jab

they pushed a little of themselves inside
so when your hand dips in it's like it's plunged
into the water of a well   where you hold

the coppery wishes of their ghosts
tight between your fingers

Imtiaz Dharker

The Piece

Mammy, throw us doon a piece. Tossed
from the third floor window, caught
before it hits the pavement. Ammi is quick,
she can do without a troop of children
from the neighbourhood tramping through the close
and up her new-washed stairs with filthy feet.

We pelt up and down the street till lamps are lit.
Grannie in the kitchen doin' some stitchin',
In comes the bogey man and chases grannie oot.
Upstairs she scrubs linoleum floors,
washes mountains of clothes and nappies,
drinks chai and sings

her loss in a language
we do not want to understand.
Mera dil yeh pukaare, aaja,
Mere gham ke sahare aaja.
We want the taste of being Glaswegian,
the thrill of *Shut yer gob* and *Ye wee besom!*

It lands like a massacre on the tar macadam,
white bread and jam streaked red.
We come back bloodied from our turf wars,
Celtic against Rangers,
Protestant against Catholic,
and never think to say, *This isn't our fight.*

A fight is a fight,
we stand shoulder to shoulder
with the neighbours' children by the middens.
Every fight is our fight. It feels right, even
when you come back up the close
with a knocked-out tooth or a bloody nose.

When we come back to her with jammy faces,
we are ready to wolf down a piece
of the other country, and never ask
what this hot tukra means
or why the language in our mouths
comes out sounding like a Punjabi song.

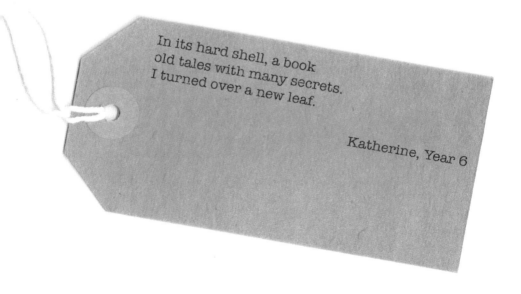

In its hard shell, a book
old tales with many secrets.
I turned over a new leaf.

Katherine, Year 6

Daljit Nagra

Letter to Professor Walcott

Hardly worth *calling them out*, the old masters.
Each time a cause gains ground, should their estate
become glass house to alleged misdemeanours?
Their body of rhyme can be felt, it propagates
its own lineage. Should we read poems from a cave,
half-witted by the missing forefather? I stand before
the compressed volumes of verse across my shelves:
who covered their tracks, who'll outlive their flaws?

Who'd topple the marble of some national bard,
or gulag their name and the chela guarding them?
How many writers, the world over, are behind bars
for crossing a border of taste? It seems natural to harm
art and the artist. Consider Larkin whose private views
were amiss, who, if akin to his father's brown shirt,
who, if published by Old Possum who laid rats on Jews...
and I've lost myself, and the Work is no longer the work.

If influence imparts bad genes, who to weigh in the scales
of my nurture? Weigh Chaucer who forced a minor
into raptus? Weigh Milton mastering tongues to bate
his women like a whip? Weigh Coleridge pairing the horror
of Othello's wedded stares to those of a black mastiff?
Weigh Whitman and Tennyson who'd cleanse by skin?
If Kipling says we're devils, may I weigh the man of "If"?
How do I edit the Frost-like swamp I've swilled –

so many poets to recycle either side of this fireplace
before sweetness and light. Before I'm woke, in tune
with the differentiated rainbow and its crying flames.
Should I calmly cease their leasehold if they've abused
the canonical fortress? Or ride a kangaroo court
on its flood of Likes? Take down each Renaissance Man
to his manhood? But I hear the poems breathe: We can't
be judged by our birth, or judge our birth as Parnassian.

And you, dear Derek. Your Adam-songs for an island
sparked paradise from sanderling, breadfruit. Your spade
dug the manor and bones fell up. The senate columns
fanfared your arrival. They donned a black male
and colour was virtue. You opened my mouth and verse
came out. Your advocates cleaned your mess, their arms
held down the age, as though gods roamed the earth
to graduate girls. As though rape were the father of art.

You were "Dutch, n____", Brit, you were my Everyman!
Why take on Caliban's revenge? Your moustache
a broom wedging its stanza of nightmare – in how many
Helens? Did you lust after lines inspired by whiplash,
taunted by sirens for your Homeric song? Intellectual
finger-jabbing seems off the mark: in the papers
Korean Ko Un's erased, and who'd fly to a terminal
if it was named for a serial pervert, Pablo Neruda?

I bet they hunt the dark man, Derek, in pantheon death.
Haunted or wreathed – how should you be honoured at
Inniskilling? Well, it seems fitting you fall in the West
where you carried "our" burden. Beside the foul spot,
I'd test my love again. You are in me: I'd never lose
you, if I tried. I'd begin with these, your old books, anew.
Now where on my shelves are you, travelling through
the old world? Where's your dog-eared *Don Juan*?

Andrew Motion

Blue Hill

The simplest way
to conquer Blue Hill
in the heat of the day

is to drive and stop
at the very foot
of the gentlest slope

and this we did
but were lost at once
in the bristling shade

of maple and pine
that only slowly
disclosed the line

zig-zagging and tossed
over grasping roots
one minute lost

the next minute found
of the sketchy path
that before its end

made us doubt the extent
of our patience and ask
what had we meant

in climbing so far
through gruesome heat
and dead still air

with plaguey flies
sipping our sweat
and buzzing our eyes

until we broke free
from the trees and saw
that jumble of scree

surrounding the top
like a giant's beard
and continued up

to find lying alone
at the very peak
a colossal stone

that had nothing to do
with our human life
except for the view

it offered to show
as we took our rest
adrift in the blue

of blue Blue Hill
including below
and picture-book still

in the sinking sun
the road and car
where our climb began.

Jean Sprackland

Next

Follow the smell of river,
take a path you never noticed before,
find a forgotten boat tied up with brambles.

Drag it over green stones
and take your chances with the splintery oars.
Destination estuary.

Curlew probing the mud for fish
have left a trail of arrows, and all you want
is to arrive in a place you do not know.

So chuck the oars and wade ashore
towards a row of wharfside shacks
alive with bright graffiti

in a language
it will take you years to learn.

PAUL HENRY

The Queue for the Kiss-gate

The festival ended aeons ago
but the queue haunts on
between two fields to a meadow.

Only a few ahead of us now,
jovial, as if the rusty clang-
clang tolled fresh vows.

A sapling thrills in the breeze
like a dog shaking off a river.
Children lose themselves in trees.

And now that we're inside
the cage, we admit to nerves.
It's late

      yet the sun confuses
the year, its glitter in our eyes
as we kiss

      neither too old
nor afraid to pass through
to the second field.

MUCH WENLOCK

When I got a job at a Telford school in 1981, it didn't take us long to decide we wanted to live in Much Wenlock: a compact town, packed with history, and a network of paths snaking across the hills. After a year we decided we'd stay, and I can't see why we'd ever move.

On a bad day it can feel a bit sleepy, but on good days there's no place like it. The Wenlock Poetry Festival was full of good days, with endless visitors reminding us how lucky we are to live here.

Paul Francis

All those lost poems
Caught up in twigs and branches
Like last Autumn's leaves

Ted Eames

Lucy Ingrams

Blaze of trails

When the number 18 shuttle hippo-ed up a ridge and windowed
over, a festival shone back at us, though I thought it was Much
Wenlock. And when someone pointed, **there,** I thought
a churchyard instead of 'poeTREE'. And, **there**, I thought
a wedding instead of 'poetry busk marquee'. The pinwheel
crowds? Shoppers. Never poets.
   The folio greens around (which I mistook for fields) smirked
at my mistaking as we lofted there, concentrating on that
concentration under Wenlock Edge. I rubbed my eyes –
hard (not yet having heard of *keratoconus*, a rubbed-eye
blindness), seeing stars. A foreshadowing...
   Before we plunged 400 feet to merge – and found the richest
kind of party. Like comets, the poems I heard next trailed
dust I've tangled in for years –

Ross Donlon

At the Much Wenlock Poetry Festival

After Breughel

As though gravity had suddenly become horizontal
patrons run from the town square,
drawn by the magnet of poetry.
Arms point, faces gawk, legs buck
as they try to run in different directions.

A woman abandons her corset of couplets,
a man fears for his postmodern codpiece,
girls and boys laugh at the upturned town
as they gaze through words to new worlds.

Wenlock Books strains at its spine,
Anna is a multi-armed deity, books waving in each hand.
Money clutchers quiver with reader fever;
the moon jumps over a cow;
Christopher Robin jumps out of the closet;
Poet Laureates dance with Parrot Lorikeets;
owls and pussycats busk with The Jumblies,
barrels of ballads roll down to pubs
already awash with sonnets.

Then Titania and Oberon agree on the weather for just three days
while Puck trails stars above the Much that is Wenlock.

Barry Tench

Wenlock

The Priory Hall, done up in its Sunday best,
has long breakfast tables laid for poets.
In the car park, a repurposed ambulance
is decked in celebration bunting.

The Methodist church pews are polished
by a new congregation; the audience waits
in respectful rows as the poet paces
the cool-light transept, speaking her verse.

A crow flies unseen over the poetry tent,
a world in which there are bales for seats,
blossoms for banners, and performers
have their timings down and well-rehearsed.

Soon evening will hum at The Edge, headliners uncap
bottles at sound check, and in the bar, volunteers
take breath. For a time, this is how our
summers passed: poetry at the heart of Wenlock.

Ian Duhig

Wenlock Old Poetry Fair

"Do you pass where they'd hold the poetry fair?
Seek my old love who I'm told wanders there:
tell him to sail to some distant country
to see can he find there the equal of me.

Say on this voyage to bottle me brine
that tastes like fresh water and not tears of mine.
Tell him on landfall to write me white land
between the sea water and the dry sand.

Tell him to plough it verse-end to verse-end,
the track of his ploughshare a fisherman's bend;
say too carve needles out of fish bone
for a coat of fresh air these needles have sewn.

Say if he does this, it's still done in vain,
for he's a vain poet I won't love again.
He has an ego instead of a soul:
where his heart should beat, I found a hole."

I called at Wenlock, as I had been told,
and sought out her poet who seemed young and old;
I gave him my message which caused him much pain;
he gave me another I brought back again:

"That hole in my heart drains my tears when I cry;
the o in my ego is that needle's eye;
absence threads needles a poet once wrote
and that's how I'd stitch the fresh air for your coat.

A mast for my journey's this I of our storm,
a pen ploughs my wake and a tongue's my craft's form;
I'd angle for fish with the north or south pole,
seek landfall to harbour a dark empty soul.

I'd bleach my page white with your brine bottle's salt
to write our lost love which is all my cursed fault.
I'm vain as my art, yes, and I'd sail lost coasts,
but my home's now Wenlock with poetry ghosts."

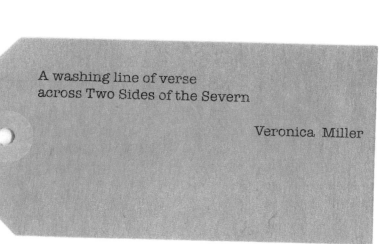

A washing line of verse
across Two Sides of the Severn

Veronica Miller

JEAN ATKIN

The Weathering of Wenlock Priory

On this houndstooth lip
     are prayers
          worn thin by rain.

         Amens have sheared
     the prior's sandstone
to this looser wool.

     A hundred decades blur
          the mason's chiselled line
              back into plough

         sown now with lichens,
     titupping like his sheep
on grainy hills.

IAN PARR

St Milburga's Priory

Cluniac

Much Wenlock, Shropshire

We are gods now
granting charity, amending
thereby these ruins' multitudinous sins;
present, past and whatever to be,
like faces we tread upon,
we see or pretend not to see.

We are gods now. These views ours.
Nowhere is holy. We tread our un-angelic
eyes and voices into history's faith
without a sigh or prayer without despair.
Nor enquire how many masons' bloodied bones
were carted off staging a hundred feet
above the nave.
We will never know even if we care.

Some few might imagine God's view
from His high altar into spangled light.
All will see aged stones
piled and fallen like obscure sinners,
timeless as ancient trees,
and long blue hills
a poet dreamt he saw.

Carol Caffrey

Little Pieces of Gold

A chest
of past treasures
open it slowly, feel
the flourish of silk brush along
your arms.

A blue
morning surprise
there's Carol Ann Duffy
outside the bakery queuing
for rolls.

Around
the corner comes
John Inverdale walking
a dog. How small he seems, John not
the dog.

He'd not
seen Leinster play
the day before, alas,
his loss. They were poetry in
motion.

Pages
of poems damp
with rain, sunshine bursting
on the green, just time to catch the
shuttle.

How kind
of a writer
friend to fix my blouse, way
too loose, before my ten minutes
of fame.

Now put
the memories
back, fold them tenderly
in your chest until you need them
again.

in a world
of change...bread and butter
pudding

David Bingham

FESTIVAL POETRY BREAKFAST

Poetry Breakfast is one of my favourite ways to enjoy poetry, and it is wonderful that this aspect of the Wenlock Poetry Festival continues, with first-Thursday-of-the-month meetings in Much Wenlock, and second-Thursday online events.

Here, in this Festival Poetry Breakfast on the page, are poets that I maybe didn't know when the Festival was happening, or just didn't manage to get hold of. How pleased I am to be able to share their poetry with you now – and what marvellous poetry it is.

My thanks to each.

Anna Dreda

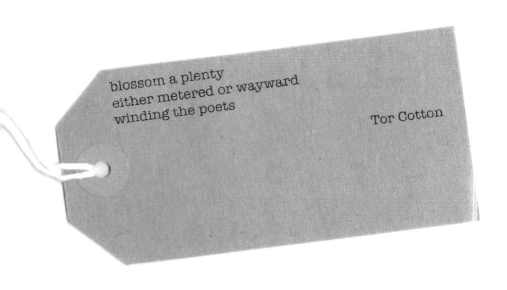

blossom a plenty
either metered or wayward
winding the poets

Tor Cotton

Kim Moore

We are coming

We are coming under cover of darkness,
with our strawberry marks, our familiars,
our third nipples, our ill-mannered bodies,
our childhoods spent hobbled like horses

where we were told to keep our legs closed,
where we sat in the light of a window and posed
and waited for the makers of the world
to tell us again how a woman is made.

We are arriving from the narrow places,
from the spaces we were given, with our curses
and our spells and our solitude, with our potions
we swallow to shrink us small as insects

or stretch us into giants, for yes, there are giants
amongst us, we must warn you. There will be riots,
we're carrying all that we know about silence
as we return from the forests and towers,

unmaking ourselves, stepping from the pages
of books, from the eye of the camera, from the cages
we built for each other, the frames of paintings,
from every place we were lost and afraid in.

We stand at the base of our own spines
and watch tree turn to bone and climb
each vertebra to crawl back into our minds,
we've been out of our minds all this time,

our bodies saying no, we were not born for this,
dragging the snare and the wire behind us.

TESS JOLLY

Bluebells

Now waking, now sleeping
      we're cradled
by the structures we built from our fear of the world,
its carnival of bramble and foxglove,
      sustained by the light we absorbed
      for as long as we could stand it
      before retreating into the safe, familiar soil
      of ritual and behaviour,
secrets kept by the undergrowth –

so what coaxes us back to the lay-bys and woods
      where the canopy of the mind still holds itself open
      and the retina is plated in that shade of blue
      that chimes – dare we say it –
      with something like a soul,
wood bell, witch's thimble, cuckoo's boots,
so much blue our hearts are drenched, euphoric?
      Not magic, not miracle,
      but endurance, desire, faith.

CHAR MARCH

Washing my mother's hair

It is role-reversal time: she's bird-thin
fragile as her brittle smile
her teeth suddenly too big for her mouth
lips thinned, clumsy with Vaseline
to stop the cracks showing.

Only last summer she broke the World Record
in Running For The Bus, carrier bags thumping
at her varicose legs, then fanned herself
with the Radio Times all the fifteen stops home.

Now her spine is hooked into a question mark
from which her head tries to look up.

For the first time in my life, and hers,
I pour the warm water, the baby shampoo,
the best conditioner I could buy, rub the blushing whiteness
of her scalp gently while she holds her flannel
clamped to her eyes like she taught me to.

And she says, *That's right, give it a good rub.*
Sure and I'll be a new woman.

And I rub and joke with her in a put-on voice:
Has Madam done her numbers for the lottery yet?
and *Will it be Torremolinos again this year, Madam?*
and the other things that mind-numbed hairdressers
say to their ladies

and nothing at all about how much I love her.

Catherine Graham

The Washing Machine

She dislikes the sound of the washing machine
so I sing as it starts to spin, willing it to stop
before she calls for me from the bathroom.

She used to love hanging the washing out,
proud to peg 'the whitest sheets in the street'
and watch them as they billowed on the line.

Sometimes, they'd be bone dry but she'd
leave them out, on show to Mrs. Ridley.
I remember how Mrs. Ridley and my mother

would stand, arms folded, like bookends
in headscarves and slippers exchanging the latest
chinwag. I remember the pleasure Mam took

in folding the bedclothes with me, how
she'd do that little dance towards me until
our fingers met, her fingers gentle and plump.

"Where are you?" she shouts from the bathroom,
"I've sat here two hours!" It's been two minutes.
I hurry along the passage, still singing 'our' song.

Keeping her face to the wall, Mam joins in.
We sing our hearts out to "Delilah",
each of us as lonely as the other.

Meg Cox

Woman's Hour

Doing some ironing one morning
I found myself listening to an interesting talk
about slim line tracksuit bottoms
but that worried me because
I knew they wouldn't suit my bottom.
After I'd learnt some useful uses
for reusable plastic bags
I listened to some women talking
about their elective labial reduction surgery –
'correct and define your inner labia'.
Unlike those other parts of my body
I have spent my life worrying about,
my bottom (see above), and my nose, and my knees,
I thought 'that part' had served me well,
and anyway… But it seemed clear
that my life might be improved, even now,
by such an up-to-date fashionable piece of equipment.
Maybe nothing would be finer than a designer vagina.

Brian Patten

Geography Lesson

Our teacher told us one day he would leave
And sail across a warm blue sea
To places he had only known from maps,
And all his life had longed to be.

The house he lived in was narrow and grey
But in his mind's eye he could see
Sweet-scented jasmine clinging to the wall,
And green leaves burning on an orange tree.

He spoke of the lands he longed to visit,
Where it was never drab or cold.
I couldn't understand why he never left,
And shook off the school's stranglehold.

Then halfway through his final term
He took ill and never returned,
And he never got to that place on the map
Where the green leaves of the orange trees burned.

The maps were redrawn on the classroom wall;
His name was forgotten, it faded away.
But a lesson he never knew he taught
Is with me to this day.

I travel to where the green leaves burn
To where the ocean's glass-clear and blue,
To all those places my teacher taught me to love
But which he never knew.

Carole Bromley

Pry'vit

Two new pupils started at our school,
Ivan and Nadiya. The Head explained
that they had just arrived here from Ukraine.
They looked so nervous; how could they tell
what he was saying? There was applause
when they walked in and I'm not really sure
why it made me cry. Mum hides the paper,
these days Daddy switches off the news,

and yet the footage haunts me anyway;
women and children, nowhere left to go,
a father puts his hand against the window
of a train. I can't think what to say;
I offer Nadiya my pen, I don't yet know
that *pry'vit* is Ukrainian for *hello*.

RORY WATERMAN

Gooseberries

i.m.

She bends back over the bush,
pursed hand biting for curvature
among the green, and rains
three more to the tub at her feet.

Then she finds a last one, hunches,
lifts and rattles her find, is gone
inside. A tractor's been pacing
the field next door all morning,
towards, back, towards, back.
She went unnoticed, unnoticing.

And we'll have gooseberry tart –
as tart as her love, its stout fruit
as coarse and hard to sense, when
hidden and wasting in its thicket.

John Foggin

Wren

God thought of the smallest coin
he could make, and made the Wren
to fit, neat as a thumb in a thimble,
tail cocked like a flintlock trigger.

He should have loved the Wren more
than let the boys come smashing down
the thorn, chanting, calling: Wren!
come out! come out! come out and die.

With her hairspring call, she can not
keep silent, the Wren, full as an egg
with alarm and urgency, her voice a tattle
of fingernails on an old tin lid.

Fragile as a chalice on its thin glass stem.
Why kill a Wren and her mid-winter song?
What did she ask for but a zipwire of air,
a tangle to hide her nest, a May full of flies?

David Constantine

The rowans of Creigiau Camddwr

Things being the way they are
Lately I've looked to trees for encouragement in lasting
With zest a while longer. From the col of Creigiau Camddwr

Descending by a stairway of small footholds
Your boots brush harebells whose own way of survival
Is lightness, dance. Pause, look across to where

The descents are the work and the paths of water in all her shapes
                          and lights
Down-ricocheting through an uproar. There
In that smithy hazed with rainbows

The tree that claims a higher life than any other in our land
The rowan, mountain ash, quickbeam, its seed
Bird-shat, stream-borne, rammed into cracks by the wind and the rain

Nurtures on very little a hard dark hope of becoming
Next summer and autumn a reminder of Eden, white, crimson. You
On your slight platform with the harebells, across the void

Fathom if you can what life that slim tree makes in a fissure. How one
Emergent reaches for the sky; another
For the horizontal; a third, the trapeze girl, trusting her roots

Flings forward her red hair and goes headlong. All
Out of the hold they have, as it allows or thwarts, unfurl
A beauty akin to freedom. All wear, however they shape themselves

The crown and glory of fruition. And all
In the rainbow clamour, in the draught of toppling waters
Shiver continuously, they make a whispering as though one final time

A needed language we have forfeited the hearing of
Were being offered us. So the rowans
Gratis display their yearly barely noticed

Never-the-same perfected selves
Fit show for an angel. And you, passer-by
Precarious witness of these lives that arise in a downfall

Knowing your kind will not resurrect like that
When you lie sleepless, failing the living and the dead
Will it not help to remember your soul is a climber of streams

And holds the clew to the rowans of Creigiau Camddwr?

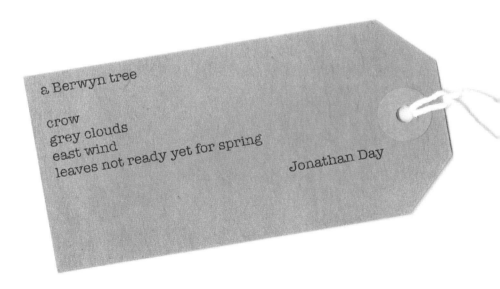

a Berwyn tree

crow
grey clouds
east wind
leaves not ready yet for spring

Jonathan Day

Amanda Dalton

The Possibility of Fog

If this long familiar road can turn
to cataract, my friend become
invisible though he still stands
at my side, if the heifer can
die from grazing air and water
as she stumbles to the barn,
if in a moment everything can
muffle, everything murmur
and cling like apparitions
in the night though it's only 2pm,
if I can be so suddenly and
spectacularly lost in the place
I was born, lost before
there's even time to watch
the bowl of the valley fill
with floss (delicate muslin
turning like those useless
curtains we used to wrap
around ourselves when we were
young and drunk), if cloud can
fall to the ground then rise
again and there's the old oak
that was gone and the meadow
grass and a spider's web and
the road all glittered with frost,
and my friend is beside me
laughing and someone has turned
the volume up and there's even
a curlew in the clear bright air,
if this is possible then maybe
everything is possible.

Kathryn Bevis

Meet me at the swings

Never give in to gravity but
suspend yourself, weightless
over that summer sneeze
of a village green in childhood. Wheel
above the wool shop with no customers,
the bus-stop with no buses. Suck

sweet-and-sour twists
of cough candy from the dusty jar
at Aunty Pat's Post Office
and Spar. Cast aside your boots
and socks, practical as fractions.
Now, flex your toes against

the air, ignoring bossy bells
and bedtimes, come-in-for-your-tea
times. Instead, release your wild
and bolting body to the rhythms of its lilt
and swoop, its lean and soar. Laugh
at a world so heavy on its feet.

WORKSHOP

Andrew McMillan

Workshops are a vital part of any festival. They feel to me as though they're many things at once: perhaps a workshop is a chance to go behind the scenes with a poet we've just seen perform and get insights into their techniques and ideas; perhaps a workshop is a social space – a chance for chat and connection away from the reverential hush that falls on an auditorium; perhaps a workshop is a space that elongates time away from the hustle and bustle of the signing table or the snatched glimpse of a favourite author. All I know for certain is that some of my best memories of festivals, and of Wenlock Poetry Festival in particular, have been around a workshop table.

People come to workshops for different reasons: some want a handy hint or a tip to help them write something; some want simply to be in a room of ideas, to talk to fellow writers at different stages of the journey; some hope to leave with something whole and intact, as though the workshop were a form of metal detection, finding a perfectly preserved artefact just beneath the conscious mind of the participant. The thing I've always felt workshops can do really well is be useful in two different timeframes at once. They might get something on the page in the moment, but then a year down the line, when we're sat on our own trying to find a new way into a poem, we might remember that thing somebody said, an idea somebody suggested to us. It might provide the key we'd been missing.

Workshop exercises, too, are always artificial. They exist because otherwise we'd just spend time talking about ideas, and they might then drift away. Exercises are a way of making something concrete, getting something down on paper. The thing we build in the workshop is perhaps a prototype, an example, something we can deconstruct and borrow the component parts of as we go through our writing life.

Writing exercises are also kaleidoscopic; each person, if the exercise is strong enough, can get something different from it. The trick, eventually, is to be able to prompt yourself, to notice something odd or interesting as you walk down the street or look out of your window and allow the connections to be made in your brain. This morning, on my way to the gym, I saw a For Sale sign propped inside a bus stop. *It looks like one of the figures in the nativity*, I thought, *hunched over in the barn, looking down at the baby Jesus.* Maybe the thought will go nowhere, maybe it will, but that's a prompt. I've set myself a writing exercise simply by being in the world and being alert. That's my challenge to you: notice something, and then hold that thing and see if it begins to grow.

PUBLISHER IN
RESIDENCE

Reading these poems takes me back, with very fond memories, to Wenlock and the buzz of poetry all around the town and in all manner of places: our first ever group of Primers poets reading together in the Pottery; Deborah Alma's wonderful Emergency Poet ambulance parked up and covered in bunting; the beautiful surroundings of Wenlock Edge; the welcoming bookshelves stacked with new collections of poetry in Anna Dreda's Wenlock Books; tea and cake in the cafe; friendly faces and late night curry with fellow writers. The being together of it all.

Jane Commane, Nine Arches Press

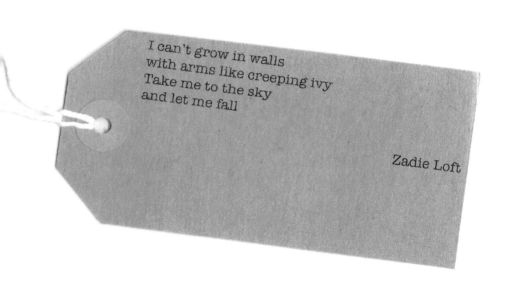

I can't grow in walls
with arms like creeping ivy
Take me to the sky
and let me fall

Zadie Loft

Deborah Alma

Venus, Goddess, Mother

after the sculpture 1.Figurine by Kevin Blockley

It's something to do with worms and teeth;
my mother said, if I didn't brush my teeth
I would start to feel the worms in them;

something to do with Mother and teeth
she said that if I didn't have my teeth,
something to do with no-one would love me

something to do with men and worms
and what my mother said, of men
and how I couldn't sleep as the worms writhed and sneaked

something to do with rot and teeth and roots
and women crossing continents
in the hands of men.

Something to do with a goddess, a Mother –
who never stood on her own two feet,
Willendorf, Hohle Fels, soft stone, sharpened pegs

of legs and teeth; something to do with how
she will not be kept grubbed in a hand, rubbed and stroked
across continents, and buried for centuries long,

with her legs that taper to a point, soft in stone;
yet still the rot of worms and men. Carved in the round,
not something unearthed. Unmothered.

Her roots of teeth.

Josh Ekroy

've been wearing it

for two hours now and not a single person notices
when I laugh in Monsoon as I read an eye-message
nor when I finger-sketch a Van Gogh sweater
in the queue at Wasabi. Even when, descending
the St Pancras escalator, I taptic with my teeth
my caller's not impressed – wait, do you mean my voice
is coming on speaker out of your mouth? And when I tell friends
first they say, I want one, then: does it work?
I say just breathe through your nose.

You can send a heartbeat, sketch an emoji and your own finger
gives you a kindly tap, closer to human contact
than a vibrate or a beep, like that close nudge you love.
You can thought-message, so all your friends have one too,
and having had insertion the next decision is which face:
scorpion; Octonauts; langur; or Dead Seas of Mars.
You don't hold your face out in front of your face,
that gauche faux-zombie posture that says
this is all we're good for now.

The act of speaking has a history that predates digital,
and it's not that comfort-blanket thing. I leave my clutch bag
knowing it will zzz if besties call. In that awkward lift moment
I have a quick look at me. And if your Dad taps when you're having sex,
and if he FaceTimes, this needs The Full Blink:
an eye-lid blanks it.

ABEGAIL MORLEY

Catching your death

In my clumsy bare-wounded way
I think of your war, the scratch-fabric you wear,
the way you say, *Albumen*, in the long drawn out tone
of someone who has seen limbs and air collide.
I dress myself as if I've stepped out of glass
and you're the only person who presses their palm,
with surprising accuracy, to the spot of me
bleeding. Somewhere in the cold lip of glass
I find myself shouting and shouting.

And a lifetime away sunlight is flocking
over your uncombed wet hair
and you're unbuttoning your expression
in the old-fashioned evening, puckering your mouth
to the iron-dark water and scurrying in the mirror
for the handful of stones to fill your pockets. You
open yourself up again and again like the mouth
of cave, a sore, surgery.

Julia Webb

Bee Dress

Give me a dress made of honeybees
that I will wear in humming praise of summer,
that shimmies its blacks and yellows
across my body in waves,
each curve of bee a buzzing bead
that catches the sun's rays as I move.

Let the whole street see my waggle dance
as my bee dress swarms and sings –
lifts me clear above the pavement,
leaving behind me a fine yellow dust,
a faint whiff of honey.

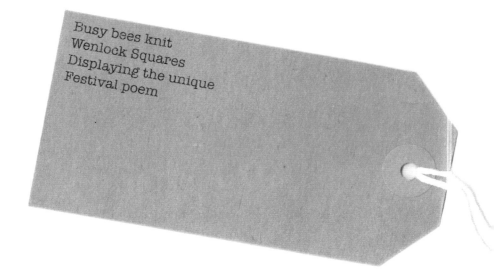

Busy bees knit
Wenlock Squares
Displaying the unique
Festival poem

Robert Peake

Summers on the River with Dad

All night, the clink of a lantern hook
then through the thin canvass, dawn
and butter burning in the pan.
What I hate about fishing is the smell.

Any other son would leap, like you,
to greet the morning with a goofy song,
but my head is full of equations
and the birdy chirp of little poems.

You hand me an oar, and we shove
into the reed beds, still as egrets
where I will whisper back as excitedly
as we both really wish I could be.

Jo Bell

From here on up all the paths are informal

At last. The roads run out in sorry stops: the tarmac
can't be arsed and no-one needs to come here but the bees.
Always, above the fishy knotwork of a seafront town
there's such a watershed of routes; a plain place
of no camber. All roads end in grass and you are forced
to make your bloody mind up and to choose –
or shrug off choice entirely, striking out for teatime
with nothing but a bag of sandwiches and half a clue
where anything might be. Anything is not the thing
in any case. The land holds onto megaliths
and hedgerows. Metalled roads, it knows,
are just a phase we pass through now and then.

Roy McFarlane

Fires of Sedgley Beacon

This is the hill they made us run up
in the moulding of our youth. Hills moulded
through pre-historic times, once festooned
with lagoons, where trilobites crawled as fast
as my weary legs could carry me. *McFarlane,*
you're lagging behind the P.E. teacher shouted.
This place marked by coral seas and icy wasteland.

Ground of claypits and limestone beneath bracken
and grass; the minerals for an industrial revolution,
this tartan hell, chained Titans blackened with labour.
The labour that brought my father to these shores
to Bilston Steel Works, seen from the Beacon Tower –
where fires were once lit for the warning of the Spanish
Armada – Big Lizzie they called her standing tall, burning
its own fires, bleeding molten gold, coughing her dark breath
into the skies as long as there was labour but the Tories came
and Thatcher closed her down. Our fathers laid off and mothers
mourned, finding ways to make *spam and payes*,
bully beef and rice last long enough for another day.

Yet, we still burned in the brightness of our youth
on late summer evenings, sliding down the *bunk*
on metal trays, after *bonking* off school for a snog
or a *bonk*. Young lovers who knew nothing of the blues
of milkwort, as we burned with passion and moulding
into each other whilst carline thistle pressed between
the leaves of our bodies. The hill was on fire
as if from the heavens, some days an upper room
of tongues; patois, Punjabi and *yam yam*
converting us all to the Black Country.

GREGORY LEADBETTER

Whisht

Come to this clipping from my hair.
Make a ring of a curl I wore.

I've told you all the truth I know
from the quietus of my pillow.

When I speak your words I feel you
like a wish blown through a candle.

*

Come to this – my bottled breath
warm enough for you to live.

I take up a feather, air-write to you
in magpie black and iridescent blue.

I swallow the pips of an apple core
to grow the godwise food you are.

*

Come to this papercut bleb of my blood
while it is here on my finger to suck.

You know what you have taken from me
better than I have senses to see.

I lay you a trail from a tomb to my door
in photographs, one for each living year.

*

Come to this seed in the palm of my hand.
I've held out my arm as long as I can.

I dry out my sweat, leave you the salt
of my fervid body, torrid or cold.

I set a fire to bring the dawn
and the far imago trying to be born.

                    *

Come – I've given all you need of me.

Spell out in silence my other name.
I hold my tongue like a flame.

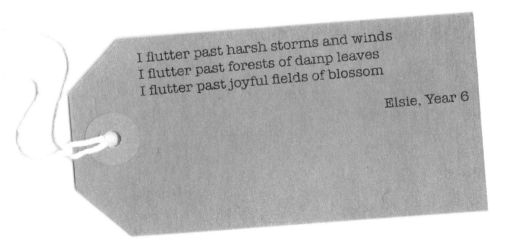

I flutter past harsh storms and winds
I flutter past forests of damp leaves
I flutter past joyful fields of blossom

Elsie, Year 6

DANIEL SLUMAN

warm milk

your bottom lip sweet with red bull

the pale crease of your collarbone
lengthening in half-light

i pour these memories into paper
as best as i can

& gather you in my arms
to drink each freckle

before we sleep deep in that dark

where my shame sits
in the corner

like my father did
when i was thin as a melon rind with the chemo

learning that the body
is warm milk

& i couldn't sleep

without knowing
he was there

just like i can't sleep now

watching my breath shake
each hair

on your neck

Isobel Dixon

March

is the month
of daffodils
in jam jars
on windowsills

slim shafts
of home-sap
greening
our sightlines

supping the tap-
draught
opening up –
to the lamp-glow

the grey pane
the generous
thermostat
winter-breath

of house moles
stirring
to consciousness –
fattening this one source

of butter-golden
hope-filled
sure and repeating
light

YOUNG WENLOCK

Wenlock Poetry Festival loved working with local children and young people in the build-up to the annual weekend, during the Festival, and throughout the year. The Festival also funded special projects within schools and hosted the Wenlock Poetry Festival Young Poet Laureate scheme.

In 2016 we had our first dedicated children's marquee decorated with hundreds of children's poems displayed as washing line bunting. We took poets and artists into schools; children created a poetry pamphlet and had the opportunity to perform their poetry at various locations and some of them created a special calendar for Cuan Wildlife Rescue. One of our projects was 'Two Sides of the Severn' linking Much Wenlock Primary School with a school in Telford (schools north and south of the River). The children worked with Jean Atkin, creating a poetry pamphlet and performing at The Edge Arts Centre.

Throughout it all, we had a thoroughly good time and send grateful thanks to all the children, teachers, parents, poets, artists, colleagues, trustees, and volunteers who had a good time with us.

Sarah Povall and Veronica Miller

The rust spread, the memories fled
I wonder, are there fingerprints
across the weatherworn handle?
Round the bucket, vines are woven,
like on the top of a pastry pie.
It is still full, in more than one way.

Toby, Year 6

ROGER McGOUGH

The Clever Chameleon

I live in a letter box
on the island of Crete
Warm in the winter
cool in the heat

Though lonely at first
life soon got better
When postcards dropped in
the occasional letter

Peace and quiet
is all that I need
Now that I'm busy
learning to read

I'm a literate lizard
in my letter-box home
And I love it so much
I've written a pome

Roger Stevens

Judy Dog's Secret

You can bribe me with treats
and biscuits and meats
but I'm not telling you
where I buried it.
You can yell, you can shout,
you can stomp all about,
but I'm not telling you
where I buried it.

You can stroke me and tickle me
under my chin.
You can say, "Just you wait
'til your mummy gets in."
You can offer me caviar
straight from the tin,
but I'm not telling you
where I buried it.

It's my favourite toy.
It's what gets my vote.
I just love to chew it.
It's what floats my boat.
I don't know what it's for
but it's called 'a remote'.
And I'm NOT telling you
where I buried it.

Emma Purshouse

To a Hedgehog in Winter

Oh spiky
fleet-footed
turner of speed
Oh cat food cruncher
twilight bringer
guardian of the half light
Oh slug muncher
gourmet of the worm feed
Oh precious furzepig urchin
I miss you, my snuffling
visitor of the scented
summer nights

Gareth Owen

Cold

I'm sidding in der garden
Ibe drying to sbell dis rose
Bud id mide as well be a donion
On accound ob diz code in by doze.

The Sound of Spring

I heard old Autumn shuffling off
I heard cold Winter going
Then bouncy Spring came leaping in
Bedoing! Bedoing! Bedoing!

In the Country

The birdy skies are filled with tweet
The fields are gold with growing wheat
The sheep say baa, the cows say moo
The farmyard's filled with pong and pooh.

Angela Topping

Where Do I Come From?

I come from a planet
more blue than green.
It has more creatures
than I've ever seen.
Some walk on two legs,
some on four.
We live on the surface –
too hot at the core.
Some fly through the air,
some swim in the sea.
Not all of us aliens
look like me.
Each end is frozen
and covered in snow,
the middle is warm
where rainforests grow.
We circle in space
and follow the sun.
There's enough on our planet
for everyone.

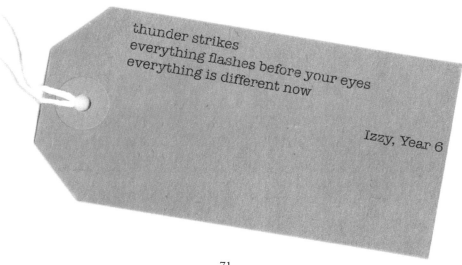

thunder strikes
everything flashes before your eyes
everything is different now

Izzy, Year 6

CHRISSIE GITTINS

Holi

A splodge of purple on your neck
and you can feel the temperature rising.

A rub of brown on your cheek
and your friend is your friend forever.

A cloud of red above your head
and your feet start itching to dance.

A scatter of yellow on your shirt
and your enemy is now your friend.

A blotch of blue on your nose
and the winter is soon forgotten.

A bucket of black down your back
and you are ready to beat the drum.

A stream of orange in the air
and your heart begins to surge.

A smear of pink on your forehead
and your misdeeds fade away.

A dusting of green on your eyelashes –
spring is surely on its way.

*Holi is a Hindu Festival known as the 'Festival of Colours' and is now
celebrated all over the world at the end of winter.*

ANDREW FUSEK PETERS

Last Night, I Saw the City Breathing

Last night, I saw the City breathing.
Great Gusts of people,
Rushing in and
Puffing out
Of Stations' singing mouths.

Last night, I saw the City laughing.
Take-Aways got the giggles,
Cinemas split their sides,
And Living Rooms completely creased themselves!

Last night, I saw the City dancing.
Shadows were cheek to cheek with brick walls,
Trains wiggled their hips all over the place,
And the trees
In the breeze
Put on a show for an audience of windows!

Last night, I saw the City starving,
Snaking Avenue smacked her lips
And swallowed seven roundabouts!
Fat office blocks got stuffed with light
And gloated over empty parking lots.

Last night, I saw the City crying.
Cracked windows poured falling stars
And the streets were paved with mirrors.

Last night, I saw the City sleeping.
Roads night-dreamed,
Street Lamps quietly boasted,
'When I grow up, I'm going to be a star!'
And the Wind,
Like a cat,
Snoozed in the nooks of roofs.

Shauna Darling Robertson

Uncle Billy is Teaching Me How to Whistle

We sit on upturned buckets in his herb garden
pulling faces at the parsley.

We foxtrot across to the Friday fish market,
stuff ourselves with sardines,
spit out the spines and scales
and stitch them into superlative silver spacesuits.

Next stop, the corner sweetshop.
We crunch our way
through seven colours of sunshine-scented candy
then rummage for pots of gold
under each other's rainbow-striped tongues.

But how is any of this helping my whistling?

Oh, that, says Uncle Billy.
The whistle will come when the whistle is ready.

So what exactly are we doing here?

Entertaining ourselves while we wait, he says
as he conducts an imaginary orchestra
with a blur of index fingers
that almost trip up a passing dragonfly.

Morar Lucas

Invaders

They came, these infants, aged but three and one
and claimed and colonised our house...our lives.
Johnny wanted everything at once – the world
explained in instant clear replies
to his endlessly recurring "whys?"
He said, at 6 a.m., "I cannot read but only look.
So, Granny, please wake up and read this book;
and Grandpa, play this game again, again, again, again."

Hugo, a wordless conqueror, briskly crawled
like a small tank, remorselessly from room, to hall,
to stairs, till with contented smiles
he homed in where the fragile things were
stashed away, and maximum potential lay
for havoc.

Now they have gone. We wander round
the exhausted house, bereft. It's quiet,
undisturbed, and sadly so are we.
But everywhere we see
a scattering of toys – a plastic hammer here,
some soldiers there – and over all
a tide of vivid grandparental joys
plus, underneath the cot,
one striped, enchanting, mini ankle-sock.

WORKSHOP

Emma Purshouse

Winter Wonderlands:

where things that don't go together sometimes do!

This activity uses **juxtaposition** which is about putting two things together that shouldn't really go, but then they do. The result is sometimes startling language that makes you go 'wow', or makes you chuckle. It's the kind of language that might work well in a poem.

Things you will need:

- Something to write with and on
- A grid on a separate piece of paper that looks like the one on the next page
- Some wintry thoughts
- A cup of hot chocolate and a biscuit (optional)

Starting point:

Think of an outside scene. Maybe a park. Or a city centre. Or a school playground. Or a wood. Or a back yard. You can imagine the scene, but sometimes it's nice to go and sit in the actual place you want to write about.

Mismatch Activity:

Now take your grid and follow these instructions:

1. Fold the paper longways with column 2 facing out towards you.

2. Fill in column 2 first. List the names of the 'things' in your scene. Put one in each box. For a park scene you might choose *slide*, *tree*, *robin*, *litter bin*, *bench*, *rat*.

3. When column 2 is full, flip over the piece of paper so that column 1 is facing you. DO NOT LOOK BACK AT COLUMN 2!

4. ERRR... I SAID DON'T LOOK BACK. STOP IT!

5. Now, still without looking back, fill out column 1 with wintry words. Put one in each box. These can be wintry describing words like *sparkly*, *glittering*, *crystallised*, or *soft*. These can be wintry sounds like *crunchy* or *crackly*. Or even wintry feelings like *shivery* or *bone-cold*.

6. When column 1 is full, open up the piece of paper so you can see both columns.

7. Read across the boxes and find your best mismatches. You might find a *sparkly slide, frozen robin, iced litter bin, shivering bench, glittering rats*.

Writing a Poem:

Using your favourite/oddest/funnest mismatches, make yourself a poem. Make it look and feel like a poem to **you**. It can be as long or as short as you like. Maybe use a little bit of repetition to hold it together. Give it a title. Here's mine:

On Winter Nights

On winter nights the moon beams down
on sparkly slides and soft trees
on crystallising robins and iced litter bins

On winter nights the moon beams down
on shivering benches and the glittering rats
scurrying this way and that in the bone-cold night

1. Wintry describing words	2. Things you might find in...
twilight sky cold winter breeze snow falls on cars	George, Year 6

PRIORY HALL

Tucked away between the church green and the Bull Ring is a solid, squat building of Wenlock stone. Once the National School, it was saved from dereliction in the 1980s and transformed into a bright community space.

The Priory Hall has been central to the town's cultural and civic life ever since, and it certainly held its own during Festival time. With the Emergency Poet's vintage ambulance parked in the old playground, the hall came alive as Festival HQ and Poetry Café, as well as providing space for workshops, and readings. What happy – and hectic – times they were!

Susannah Stapleton

The Garden asks: what are you Robin?
And Robin answers -
I am the blossom on the trees in April
I am the twitter in the air on a winter's day
I am the colour on an empty canvas
I am the whistle in the wind.

Molly, Year 5

HELEN MORT

Robins

for Trey

thanks to you   pal
I see robins everywhere
beady Christmas harbingers

rosy baubles strung on thin air
making cold days
feel important

and noticing   how could I not
love them   how they only blush
with their puffed out chests

spend seconds
perching on the fence   –   no rest
     they're too wicked

gossiping skywards
cocking   their heads
not truly shy

just trading on mystery
I can't ignore   the way
they lead me down the garden path

making everything
their element:

bramble   earthworm   slate

how   – even now –
they pop up when they're most needed
least expected

stern flutter   shrug of
     it'll be reyt

Alison Brackenbury

Unpeeled

Inviting me, the peach lies on the plate,
sliced dripping gold, and roughly veined with red.
The stone is broken from its bed,
the soft skin curls. I hesitate.
Hot waves of summer's scent
ripen the glowing world where day is spent
in orchards with the juice-stained pickers' gang
with sweat and longing for the winter's tang,
while perfect, undesired, the peaches hang.

Clare Shaw

Fishing for Trout in a Peculiar River

Then I met you. Our hands were touching.
Then there was light, your face was shining.
Then we were kissing

and then we were on the bed
and the fish were everywhere, twisting and flashing,
our arms were full of them

then we were sleeping.
Then there was a black night split by lightning,
a tall dark house with the lights all blazing

we were drinking
and the ceiling was full of stars
and the fish in our fists and our mouths all

gasping, the carpet was soaking
there was such a splashing
and thrashing and gorging

till the fish were all gone but the river kept singing.

ADAM HOROVITZ

Bat Racing at Summer Solstice

Tonight is the night for racing bats
on empty lanes where insects swarm
away from their usual habitats
over softened tarmac, still sun-warm.

An empty road on the solstice night
is a hedged-in tunnel of alluring heat.
No bat will be bothered to avoid your light,
so dazed are they by *all-you-can-eat*.

So mount your bicycle, ride out swift
as the sun sinks like a chequered flag.
Bat-racing is midsummer's gift;
a cooling close to the long day's lag.

Tonight let your bike be a pair of wings
and the squeak of its brakes a sonar song.
As horizons burn with the sun's last rings
race with bats through an insect throng.

Don't try to win. The race has no aim
but to follow the plunge of bats in flight
as fast as you can until summer's flame
is swallowed whole by the shortest night.

LUKE WRIGHT

Peak

To run the common path through
Jesus Green towards the Cam as first
light flits across the water. To see
your dog breathe before you on dark
March mornings. To hit the river path.
To sweat and pant. To grind the grief
beneath your feet. To get home,
tendons singing, lungs ablaze, the boys
at breakfast: radio, tea, toast,
the four bikes in the hall. Are these
the days? And if they are, how
long? How long at most?

The Night asks: what are you Bat?
And Bat answers –
I am the skin of midnight
I am the skimmer of water
I am the murderer of midges

Robert, Year 5

MARIO PETRUCCI

for an imminent daughter

our bluest Drop

because of You
our sky
is Ocean in suspense

Stars
flick tails among the Souls
that swim

our every Planet : a white
whale You skim
upon so

Sun &
Moon may fuse to become
this – Your

heart
& Skin – in that truest
Sea

You have made us
let there Be
no rule

only One
Beloved do not
refuse

Your Own
deep
blue Drop – O

Thou
unschooled
so Unstoppably So :

be You
Bluest Love
Be

You

STEVE GRIFFITHS

Son

It's strange
and poignant to the heart
to be the father to an adult man.
To have cast the die,
however you did,
to see the consequences walk
on two legs and love as they may,
which is much,
to observe the flourishes
and the mistakes
that make the heart contract
and always will, that he ran
too fast down a hard hill,
then to see how he works
in the world, held in respect
beyond your lapsed control.

Who in turn has a son
he steers and cherishes.
A siren dawns on my grandson,
it shrieks and fades, a favourite,
and he makes a delicate high
song of his own with it.

STEVIE RONNIE

The Kindness

How we nest the back seat with pillows,
our duvets descending into roads –
my three-year-old legs are kicking
your five-year-old legs that kick back –
my pyjamas tight around my wrists
I settle into sleep, dreaming about
that secret door in the sombre night.
All of this! All in my head expecting,
oh, to half-wake and be hoisted by Dad.
Instead: lights, sirens, the kindness
of blankets and us all (without Dad)
together in the damp ambulance,
Mam holding your hand and weeping –
the blood like paint on your little face.

The blood like paint on your little face.
Mam holding your hand and weeping
together in the damp ambulance
of blankets and us all without Dad.
Instead: lights, sirens, the kindness.
Oh! To half-wake and be hoisted by Dad!
All of this all in my head and expecting
that secret door in the sombre night –
I settle into sleep, dreaming about:
my pyjamas tight around my wrists –
your five-year-old legs – that kick-back –
my three-year-old legs are kicking –
our duvets descending into roads –
how we nest the back seat with pillows.

Menna Elfyn

Y Goeden ellyg, Y Mans, Pontardawe

(er cof am fy mrawd Geraint, fu farw Chwefror 13, 2022)

Fel fy mrawd mawr, doedd neb
yn dringo canghennau'n well na thi;
yn ein perllan i fyny fry oeddet
ymysg y gellyg, dy draed ar astell,
yng nghôl y golfen bêrs a'th drem
drwy ddellt i'r wybren, uwch dy ben.

Rhwng nef a daear oedd dy febyd yno
a'th feddwl ymhell, ti'r glaslanc tal
a'r gorwel yn dy alw ato gan bwyll
bach, ac at ffydd, i'th achub rhag cwymp:
gorseddfainc gras a ddaeth i'th dywys
at y Groes ysgarlad ac at Bren y Bywyd.

A bellach, rwyt wedi esgyn i dir uwch –
dy ddringfa i'r Noddfa, o'r ddaear i'r nef
yn llaw dawel yr Un sy'n estyn ei drugaredd
gan dy ollwng o'r ardd a'r goeden deuluol:
dwyn ffrwythau ddaw i'w cynnal – cynhaeaf
llawn sudd melys, pob peren a fu ac a fydd –
                              yno'n *geraint.*

MENNA ELFYN

The Pear Tree, Manse, Pontardawe

(i.m. Geraint Elfyn Jones)

As my big brother, nobody climbed
branches better or further than you;
in our orchard, high above, there you were
in the midst of pears, feet on a plank
in the arms of the boughs, looking
through a canopy to the sky above.

Between heaven and earth, just a boy,
but your mind faraway, you the tall lad
with the horizon calling you to safety
towards faith and save you from a fall:
Grace's throne came and led you to
the Scarlet Cross, and the Tree of Life.

And now, you have reached that higher land
as you climb to its shelter from earth to heaven
in the still hand of One who extends his mercy,
releasing you from the garden and your family tree:
bearing fruit in plenitude – a harvest full of sweet
juice, each pear so succulent for those – he loved –
yn Geraint. *

* His name, Geraint, means kith, kin, and friends.

SEAN BORODALE

The Death

From this bed with its wires and its ability to be leant up
and its thin blankets, cushions and attendants,
I could almost wind and fling out a stone, my slingshot
carrying a thread over its precipice
which is the edge into the dark wet stone
which is towards the ocean.
I feel I have the energy and I call, bring me the sea!
Cold grave Atlantic, what will you do with me?
What do you want?
An hour, two hours by road, I remember the way
between the little houses, Aughrim, Lough Rea.
I can go faster, my electrons
quick as Schrödinger's cat
whirling in the heat and the expanse to lose me and gain me.
They are lighting the candles of my teeth,
a small skull-hole lantern.
They are putting my keepsakes away,
as small, as slight as the arrhythmic heart-noise I was unable to keep.
Is this my family, like the sound of reeds hissing and trembling?
My heart, my liver, my body,
it was racked and hard but as soft as velvet.
It has a fine knap, my body, sun-bleached and fraying.
And here and there, they are lighting my bones.
How they burn with a small flame at the joints.
Bones that know how to burn made of hard cold wax.
Doldrums, lodes of sands blown over the bars,
here are the dunes of flesh.
I didn't know I was so scattered.
Grains of me blowing back west, making a noise
like many piped flutes, a fume of song,
the fluted noise of a lady with her head
coming apart like a nest of leaves.
What was in there after life?
Mice. Even the mice have fled.
I have been in this East too long.

I escaped in my hospital gown once,
in the vault of its bruised indigo smock;
it was like wings and only the grinding stars
cut at me and polished me thinly and quietly.
So I burned and glittered when they brought me
to the close-up incidence of the cleaners
doing the floor back to its shine, back to die again.
They make shining ground here
and wheel me across it.
It is their floor, and in it the reflections
go down to their daughters
who lie cold and pale holding other children
close to their ribs.
I lie slumped and distorted, as if I am melting.
My head lolls on its neck
like an old carnation or a dahlia flower
and my mouth is a black centre-point
they feed a banana to.
It is all I can do to chew toothlessly.
They must be my teeth on the ledge.
The glimmerings by the cards and the grapes.
And then, out there
is the place they escape with me to.
I am already beyond them, chattering
in a sack of the ground settling for the deep.
Where shall I sleep, boneless, fleshless?
My pure mind of red ruby passion, it will be enough.

Luke Kennard

Report

It would come to you,
a sad article read half-asleep
to stamp your day into the dirt
before it started, and
if you didn't want music –
the bassline through the wall,
the high-hat hissing
between the floorboards –
it would come to you,
style or key irrelevant,
a man thumping the piano;
it could be your current
favourite song, it could be
your current interfering
with the normal operation
of the heart muscle,
but it would come to you
in your own words:
yes; it has come to this!
or it would come to you
like a long report into a report
or a toasted cheese sandwich
wrapped in grease-proof paper
passed hand to hand
from canteen to corridor to
counter, down a long line
of underused hands
to you, to prepare for
the possibility – prepare ye, etc. –
it would come to you like
good teaching which is really
only the sensitisation
to prepare to recognise it
should it ever come, but it would
come to you whether
you were prepared
to recognise it or not.

FIONA SAMPSON

The Poet Vasko Popa at Grebenac

Everything I am you are
and banks of wild grass
lean into the summer wind
lean to the lens like a message

it is a black and white world
but even here lovers climb
as if you remembered them
raising their faces to the photographer

beyond whom the unseen
plain which each of them must know
has already gone on for miles

THE BUSK

Wenlock Poetry Festival featured slams, open mics, and, for two years, its unique Busk. Headline poets read alongside first-timers. Audiences came and went, stopping by between other events. The Busk was a democratic marathon, and I loved introducing its range of voices.

The mix of poetry and music was the Busk's magic, and I was delighted the afternoon LiTTLe MACHiNe popped in. They were appearing that evening on the main stage, and their settings of famous poems performed up-close and acoustic energised the Busk space.

In this section, poetry and music again sit side-by-side. A new song has been composed for *Festival in a Book* by John Hegley, and you can be present at its first public performance. Take a seat, grab a smartphone and point its camera at the QR codes, or type **bit.ly/TheBusk** into a browser. Sit back and relive a little of the Festival vibe.

Liz Lefroy

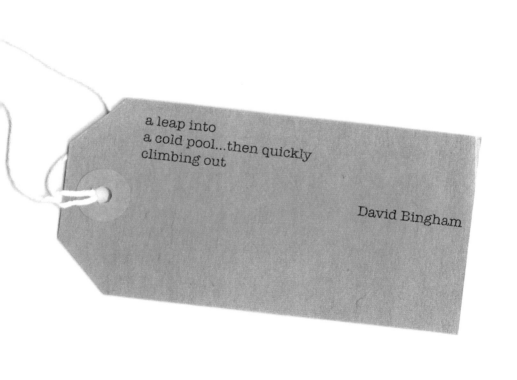

a leap into
a cold pool...then quickly
climbing out

David Bingham

Helen Kay

Quiet Please

A monthly flight of emotion. Writers
cluster in bookshops, cafés, council
cupboards. Numbers wax, wane, wax.

Butterfly words fill dark corners,
scaly skinflakes of themselves,
now colourful, now so delicate.

Moths are drawn to the mic's bulb,
need a soft hand, but drunks guffaw
and coffee machines clank and hiss.

Icy air, hard seats and jibes that poets
don't spend enough, don't bring in
the crowds, force them to move on.

Soon their bright nomadic wings
are closed notebooks, closed lips
and their words an endangered species.

Most rooms carry on their clatter
and babble; others garner chitin-dust,
ache for the age of lepidoptera.

HOLLIE MCNISH

dressed like that

we got excited getting boobs
balanced apples in our bras
to see what we might look like as women

we tried on dresses our mothers wore
when leaving late at night
or when crisps were put in bowls

smeared pink lipstick round our lips, laughed
did fashion shows in overgrown high heels
checked out our poses in the mirror

the main thing i remember
was the fun of it, how glorious
to feel our bodies growing into bodies

of people we saw doing things we couldn't:
the world, one giant party that awaited us
we giggled, practising our pouts

and everybody laughed,
until we tried to leave the house

Holly McNish

dressed like that

Paul Henry

The Glass Aisle

Nadia Kingsley

Accomplice

It was the precision of the trap.
It was wired up to spring, not at first contact
but only on victims that seemed willing.
It was the patience in the waiting.
It was the wide-mouthed grin.
It was how it tightened if they struggled
but permitted life if deemed too thin.
It was the slow, cold decomposition,
ten days of chemical digestion.
I've always kept this murderer close,
watched with growing ambition.
But since moving to a well-sealed house
I have started setting ambushes of my own
so as to keep my precious Venus flytrap pristine.

Thirza Clout

A Terrible Resolution

This is the year I must declutter – not in a kiss-arse
every sock gives me joy kind of way,
not in a tidy house tidy mind smug-arse kind of way,
not in a bloodless tight-arse minimalist kind of way;
I shall declutter in a totally bad-arse kind of way.

This will be the year I rip the guts out of ancient carcasses
kept mouldering too long in the dark under my bed.
This is the year I smash every cup and saucer Granny left
just as cracked and crazed as she was at her end,
burn unread all the letters from my father my mother kept
blaze them on a bonfire – make them vanish into ash.

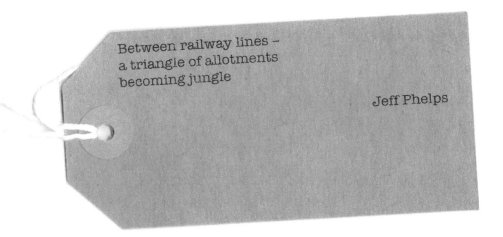

Between railway lines –
a triangle of allotments
becoming jungle

Jeff Phelps

Jen Hawkins

Border Woman

What if who you are now
is not who you used to be?
Familiar paths no longer serve.
Being off the beaten track feels best,

cliff strider, hill walker, border traveller,
shape shifting, tongue twisting,
self-forming, liminal space straddler,
off the map, in unknown territory.

Horizon dips, blurs, blends
sea sky charcoal smudge, curves
out of reach, beyond perception,
traces lands, charts continents.

Feet firmly path planted
surety, confidence of stride

ever forward facing, not back.

What's gone before cannot be undone.

Paths need no waymarked
nominer or border stone,
foot forged, heart led,
bright beacon blazed trail,
our way.

Ted Eames

vapour trail

down along the snowbound lane
I see the tracks your car left
                           already thaw-blurring
like the vapour trails we watched
yesterday
              necks arching
as parallel jet-lovers
arose in silence
                    from behind the mountain
coasting across blue-bitter skies

later their narrow white plume streams
peeled apart
                  draped and drifted
softened into paths
                     as fat and rippled
as the wake of a summer rowing-boat

your tyres have compacted this slush
I stoop to gather a tread-mark pebble of ice
                    and another
                      and another
store them carefully in a pocket
as if they will not melt

Tor Cotton

Ón mbarr

Don fhile is fearr liom...

Offering patchouli and sweat to the birdsong breeze.
Caterpillar bus, dinky and slow, on its languid trail beneath me.
Nurtured and enveloped by my barren pinnacle.
Home barely visible in my shadow.
My déagóirí remain busy with Orpheus, not a peep.
The words of "Dúchas" flutter around me on the wings of a virginal moth.
I sit with Bríd on the cusp of spring.
I am home.

Ón mbarr – From the peak
Don fhile is fearr liom – To my favourite poet
Déagóiraí – Teenagers
"Dúchas" – A poem in *Deleted* by Dairena Ní Chinnéide (who happens
to be my favourite poet)

Mary Cunningham

Passing Muse

Steve Pottinger

To make a glass butterfly

Dairena Ní Chinnéide

Ag Taibhreamh ar Chúirt na Sí

Ar imeall na hoíche
Idir dhá lios sí
Cloisim macalla na mairbh

Díbeartach mé
Crochta i líontán draíochta
Áit atá an fhírinne ina tost

Le breacadh an lae
Bristear an gheis
Is mé lom, fuar

Caite i lár leasa
Ag cosaint na fírinne
Ag árdach mo sciath

Ag lorg éisteacht

Ach ní ann a thuilleadh do chúirt na sí
Is ionam féin atá an bhrí
Léamh leochaileach ar chuimhní an chroí.

Dairena Ní Chinnéide

Ag Taibhreamh ar
Chúirt na Sí

110

DAIRENA NÍ CHINNÉIDE

Dreaming of the Fairy Court

On the cusp of the night
Between two fairy forts
The songs of the dead cry

I am an outcast
Suspended in a magic web
Where my story is silenced

Day dawns
The spell is broken
I lie cold and bare

Collapsed in the middle of the fort
Protecting my truth
Raising my shield

Seeking a hearing

But the fairy court no longer convenes
The meaning is all within
A delicate interpretation of what the heart remembers.

Sally Crabtree

The Runaway Teeth

Martin Figura

Philip Larkin on meeting
Martin Figura

MARTIN FIGURA

Philip Larkin on Meeting Martin Figura

I clutch my complimentary glass of piss.
Next time she proffers an idea   I'll ignore her.
I'll never forgive Monica for dragging me to this.

Local poets stand in clumps, all keen to kiss
my fusty arse. I wince a smile like some   ghastly vicar.
I clutch my complimentary glass of piss.

Is it Sodom, is it Gomorrah, no it's Diss
and I'm trapped in a corner with   Martin Figura.
I'll never forgive Monica for dragging me to this.

Figura explains my poetry and though he misses
by a mile, the witless crap could not be   surer.
I clutch my complimentary glass of piss.

I'll say this of Mum and Dad, for all their deficiencies
they never fucked me up, quite so much as   Martin Figura.
I'll never forgive Monica for dragging me to this.

Perhaps someone could fetch a razor for my wrists?
He proposes a book swop, O shut your box   Pandora!
I clutch my complimentary glass of piss.

Now he has the mic, but unlike Aurora Borealis
there's no good time to witness   Martin Figura.
I'll never forgive Monica for dragging me to this.

How best describe him, like deep-vein thrombosis
a clot, hard to ignore, a dreadful line without   caesura.
I clutch my complimentary glass of piss.
I'll never forgive Monica for dragging me to this.

LiTTLe MACHiNe

Jabberwocky
(Words by Lewis Carroll)

Martin Thomas

I Am
(Words by John Clare)

John Hegley

Once There Was a Festival

WORKSHOP

Jonathan Edwards

Dream Festival

One of the things I most loved about the Wenlock Poetry Festival was its fantastic sense of community, togetherness, and friendliness. It was there where I first met many people who have become fast friends, first discovered the work of new poets I've come to love, first saw in the flesh writing heroes who I'd only known on the page. There was such a positive, supportive, and happy atmosphere at the Festival, such a connection between poets and audiences. I can remember weekend mornings of driving towards the Festival and getting happier by the mile!

As a result, I wanted to make a writing prompt which was about celebrating community. Poetry of course has a long tradition of being about 'I', but it can be supremely interesting when it's about 'us', and this prompt will encourage poems which do exactly that.

The presiding influence on this prompt is Stephen Knight's amazing "The Big Parade", the opening poem from his landmark 1996 collection, *Dream City Cinema* (Bloodaxe). The poem describes a surreal, carnival-style procession through Swansea of 'everyone I've ever known/and some I've only seen on television'. When the poem says this, it means *exactly* this, going on to describe how the procession includes schoolteachers from the past, ghosts and love interests, as well as celebrities like Adam West and The Monkees, creating an unlikely and fantastic visual spectacle as the procession moves through the streets.

With this in mind, I want to invite you to write a poem about a big community event. This could be a poetry festival, an open-air concert, a dance, a visiting fair, an awards ceremony, a theatre performance, a sports event, a school reunion, a street party...any big event where people get together and enjoy themselves.

It's completely up to you who comes to the event, and this is where the fun part comes in, because you can invite *anyone*: people lodged in your memory who you haven't seen for years, long-lost friends and family members, folks who are dead and gone who you'd like to come back, as well as an unlimited cast of the talented and famous. Shirley Bassey, Frida Kahlo, William Shakespeare, Diego Maradona... It's your party, and anyone you like can show up to your event!

When writing your poem, some of the following might be useful:

- Start with a description of the event, location and what's going on, so the reader knows where they are.

- Describe each of the people in turn, what they look like, what they're wearing, and what they're getting up to at the event. What sort of fantastical things are happening?

- If it's a sporting event, is your old P.E. teacher sitting in the stands, shouting? Is George Best running up and down the touchline, trying to get onto the pitch? If it's a concert, is your grandmother standing with a baton in her hand, conducting the orchestra? Is the bloke who stands behind the counter at the local corner shop playing the tuba? Focus on actions, people interacting, folks doing stuff.

- A realist setting works well – the local playing fields or streets or school hall. Having all these fantastical figures appear in a real and down-to-earth setting can be really effective, and the poem might even be as much about your home town as the amazing things happening in it.

- Think about the ending of your poem. How does the event end? In anarchy and joy? In quiet? With a big clean-up? What emotional position has the poem got to, as a result of all the imaginative things it's shown us? What big subject have you been aiming all this at?

Hopefully, this should be a fun poem to write, where the imagination can lose itself and the writing becomes part of the pleasure of the vision you're creating and enjoying as a writer. Some pretty amazing things might happen at the event, and then all the writing has to do is record them. Sit and watch what happens, and by the detail in your writing, let us watch it too.

When the poem is finished, it would be great to complete the cycle of community, by reading it to your local poetry group, or at an open mic. Hopefully the poem you create will be one that stretches its arms wide, in all sorts of ways. I hope this prompt helps you create a poem and a writing experience which is truly in the spirit of the friendliness and togetherness of the Wenlock Poetry Festival!

Minutes before his reading, a
phonecall to Andrew Motion
announced his knighthood.
He'll certainly remember Much Wenlock.

Robert Petty

the truest voice
in the choir...
can't tell who it is

David Bingham

BORDERLANDS

There is something magical about borderlands, about liminal space that is here and there – but not quite here or there. I love living in Shropshire yet on the borders of Herefordshire and Wales, lands where borders have wandered, taking language back and forth.

I look at blue hills and think about how so many poets have remembered them.

Liz Roberts (aka poet Thirza Clout)

A friendly meeting place, friends and
families drawn together from
N / S / E / W to immerse in perfect poetry.

Lorna Taylor

Ian McMillan

Mobile

I am on the tram. It is not a real
Tram, it's a tram of the mind,
Crossing borders, calling at halts

That are more like semi-colons than
Full stops; crowds crowd on: jackets,
Skirts, a man dressed as a bear,

Someone carrying a tiny dog, someone
Holding a saxophone. This is not a real
Tram but the music is real. The power

Of art, you might say. The tram is rattling
Towards the end of the line. A bear
Gets on, dressed as a man, sits down

Because all borders are porous or should be,
Even the bear/man/man/bear border.
I get off. It's my stop. My full stop.

After that (look!) the line goes on

Fred D'Aguiar

Salmon Run, Shrewsbury Weir

for Geoff and Peter

We stared for salmon swimming home up the Severn
to this point: a foot-drop, three-step, ladder of water,

turned white under duress, stirred by the plunge,
shaken by the fall, thrown to the depths with noise.

We looked hard to catch the lucky brute, just one,
that achieves the impossible: a salmon run and jump

over the water hurdle, but could not see fish approach,
camouflaged by dark ground that the current twisted

ropey, swollen, knotted, in a constant drive from sight,
our eyes grabbed by flux and drawn back and forth.

In the middle of our search, something burst free,
leapt clear of its element, sprang from the trap

set by the weir: salmon, all arc, twist and light,
as if water stood, flexed, and all fish had to do

was climb, in a push and pull to left and right,
for this upward crawl, and lucky drown in air,

climb and come to a standstill, for a stretched
instant, only to fall, back into water's embrace,

the clutch and drag of the current, to disappear
downstream, we guess, exhausted, to regroup,

catch breath, know why it ended here, and what it
always was for: another charge at scaling the weir,

one more fling, free of the grip of the current, out, up,
head, body and tail, flying above running water, defiant.

124

Anna Selby

What Happens to Your Heart

It goes like this:
you will be floating
your skin will become thirst.
Submerge your face
a metamorphosis starts
blood retreats, heartbeat slowing
your mind an almost-state.
If you choose
dive, the transformation
grows. You become water
mammalian. On land
the equivalent pressure
kills. For the first few feet
your lungs are buoys, afterwards
contracting air shrinks you
go deeper, you swim
into a gravityless space
here is where the ocean
stops pushing you away
further, the pressure trebles
the Master Switch kicks, your heart
ticks even slower, below
it plummets – 14 beats
or lower, you should be unconscious
your chest size halves, organ walls
work as release valves.
Now, turn back up.
Everything switches
re-inflates, races.
You are land again, of and on.
Your heart broke laws.

Rosie Shepperd

"Cold is the ground"
(Blind Willie Johnson)

I know, it's hard to believe; all that time, the trailers were there, in among that little run of birch. You remember how we saw them bend and straighten their silver shadows. And you said to listen out for the way they hum their own breeze. They do. Like bottles or chimneys or paper whistles. And, after a storm, I find curls of bark in the tall grass. I have them here in a blue glass dish I call my whistling plate.

I'd like to say the trailers were far from the orchards; that I had to squint to see them; that maybe I only thought they were there. It's late now and the fruit lies all around; brown and dead but not dying. Not in that way, anyway.

I saw them again as I felt the 4/4 time of my boots on the track; picked up an echo here. Another there. A skiffle from the millstream gate as it shut; another in the 3/4 quiver of the stile as I climbed; more in the touch of each willow I brush; more again in ferns that hang and swing out quavers without thinking. I love the 12-bar; 1, 4, 5. Or I, IV, V. All abstractions matter; those that lie in the distance between a sharp and a flat and those that hide, in the farewell movement from major to minor. E♭ major, E♭ minor, E♭ minor, E♭ major.

I want to say there were three or four trailers, like I'm not counting the rolls of bedding against each pane of glass. Most of the frames are split and overlap themselves, like the scales of some great animal, old and alone; just a heap of dark limbs becoming darker.

One door is held in place with strips of tape; a stack of stuck blocks, under one corner. That lichen on the roofs; I've seen it in other places. It is lit from somewhere that isn't within and it shines up stones till they become stonier. Over there, it rounds the round pond, while here it is something else again.

I wish I could say the trailers are beautiful. Like the end of Blind Willie Johnson, who went to sleep under newspapers in the burnt out shell of his home. Not quite beautiful, and so much more. I hear his paper lungs, his cigar box guitar. I catch the bitterness of a caramel hum in the filigree of leaves. I feel brass wires, stretched and plucked like they're melting into D♭ minor, like they chose it.

Oil waits on pools of water between the great dark cuts of tractor tracks. They tremble between one colour and another. Pink and green and yellow, under the low, cold sun. I walk away and they move a little, and then a little more and they do not understand their being there.

Emily Wilkinson

Lost and Found

Our man-made maps hang heavy
as drapes over furniture of land,
yet ascend in ridged seconds
to describe the contours of crags.

Rivers wind to seam deep valleys
as blue lines fray into waterfall gush,
spit cold clear threads spun
from slate pockets of mountains.

Awkward angles are there to help
unwrap the gift of difference;
to navigate a gathering language
of rise and fall, dressmaker's marks

that size you down to less
than a pinprick in all of this.
Tiny stitches in endless tapestry
form embroidered into earth,

our true breathing body –
where every rock, fern and lichen
is woven, listening to you
trying to read the story.

Suzanne Iuppa

Territories

The overpass unravels its usefulness at night
underneath a fox cough and the cows lowing:
a lit ginnel between A-roads and B-roads

that took many messy and stop-start years to complete,
bordered by LED antennae, and in places, ancient hedgerows
hanging on for dear carbon-saving life –

and as the stars split the blackness
and swagged gardens call out from either side, familiar,
there is a shift down to a chorused humming

behind hermetic seals; through double-cylinder door locks
while the clipped grass field at the edge of the park
shimmers endlessly, just like the desert.

ocean's heart
muggy cloud cascades
thrashing winter waves collide
ocean's heart
camouflaged from desperation

Halle, Year 6

GILL McEVOY

The Shropshire Carol

The fox is deep in his lair,
he has smelled the snow on the air.

Candles and fires,
and spicy mulled wine,
holly and spruce,
ivy and pine.

Horses are standing their backs to the wind,
sheep are huddling tight in the field.

Candles and fires,
and spicy mulled wine,
holly and spruce,
ivy and pine.

Light all the fires against the dark days,
build up the fires and gather within.

Tomorrow the hills will be silenced in white,
frozen and still, the Snow Queen's long night.

Candles and fires,
and spicy mulled wine,
holly and spruce,
ivy and pine.

Lucy Rose Cunningham

Remembering

October,
when we walked and spoke of folk songs
as a prompt for making,

thought of marks in the landscape;
presence and absence,
the bodily trace of brush.

To Wenlock Edge,
limestone escarpment last trod at 18.
Think of final school year,

parties, laughter,
the woods in trouble.
Sat on the roof of an outhouse,

hypnotic fire pit below,
friends drawn round.
Living Shakespeare's Midsummer.

Recalling me and you / old friend / old lover,
youth's first taste of longing.
Coasting sun-licked roads

and sleeping in the back of a car
waking red-cheeked to limbs entwined.
Warm scent of another's skin pressed close.

October,
when we last met at the festival
I was lost; you, a muddled Dream.

CHRIS KINSEY

A Narrow Road to the Mid North

i.m. Graham Attenborough
(words in italics are from his *Absurd Ape*)

'Days and months are travellers of eternity.
So are the years that pass by' – Basho

This year you left with the swallows –
today you're my companion up Nant Gleiniant
invisible and loud as the robins singing behind leaves.
Doc Martens are fine for tramping the steep lane
sweating with drizzle. The rusty gate to the wood
is shut by shale-fall and bound by brambles –
so many ways lost through not walking.
It's easy to skip the odd starburst of cow shit
and celebrate an animal freed from the crush.
We rise out of the oak cwms, past birches
and scrub willow to where fields grow rushy
and gorse flames eternal.
Autumn claims altitude early: hawthorns
and rowans phoenix from burnt off leaves.
Rosehips remind me of a time you turned up
glamorous in lipstick, lace, and top hat.
Carno Moor's windmills spin low cloud to floss
concealing fighter jets but not the snarl
of their thrust or the growl of combustion.
Now and then, light lances cloud, exposing
vast chicken sheds, sneaked into contour lines,
betrayed by their silos and militant security.
I look, and look away, flinching at what we
do to creatures: *When animals weep*
the world will drown in tears – your words set the
Severn valley awash. I want to ask you,
'Does death remove the pain?'
I see you migrating free beyond vexations
and spot you a bouquet of betony, yarrow
and meadowsweet, broken into flowering late
by the mower's blade.

David Whyte

The Well

But the miracle had come simply
from allowing yourself to know
that this time you had found it,
that some now familiar stranger
appearing from far inside you,
had decided not to walk past
it anymore; that the miracle
had come in the kneeling to drink
and the prayer you said,
and the tears you shed
and the memories you held
and the realization that in this silence
you no longer had to keep
your eyes and ears averted
from the place that could save you,
and that you had the strength
at last to let go of that thirsty,
unhappy, dust-laden
pilgrim-self that brought you here,
walking with her bent back,
her bowed head
and her careful explanations.

No, the miracle had already
happened before you stood up,
before you shook off the dust
and walked along the road
beyond the well, out of the desert
and on, toward the mountain,
as if home again, as if you
deserved to have everything
you had loved all along,
as if just remembering the first
fresh taste of that clear cool spring
could lift up your face
to the morning light and set you free.

WORKSHOP

Jean Atkin

A Hat-Full-of-Feathers:
Making poems out of dialect

Dialect provides a rich and fascinating source of words. Here are some ideas for making poems from the dialect of Shropshire.

All the words below are sourced from the 1879 'Shropshire Word-Book' by Georgina F. Jackson, who gathered hundreds of them from all over the county and set them out with their meaning in standard English, and then their provenance. I made use of her Word-Book to write 'Fan-peckled' (Fair Acre Press, 2021).

Now it's your turn!

BARLEY-CHILD
A child born in wedlock, but which makes its advent within six months of marriage; as barley is six months between sowing and harvesting. Much Wenlock, Acton Burnell.

BED-HILLIN
A 'home-made quilt'; covering for a bed. Wem.

HAT-FULL-OF-FEATHERS
The nest of the Long-tailed Titmouse. Oswestry.

HUDDIMUKERY
Close; sly: as in hiding away money or valuables of any kind. Wellington.

PEA OF THE EYE
The pupil of the eye. Ellesmere.

WOOLERT
An owl. Clun.

SOUL-CAKE
A dole-cake for All Souls Day, of light dough, sweetened and spiced. Wem.

SCATTER-CORNER
Diagonally, as in directions across a field. Wilderhope, Corvedale.

First, read and enjoy. Then choose one word/phrase that in your mind has a story to tell. You could use that word/phrase as the title for your poem, with the definition and provenance as sub-title.

Next, consider the day, the weather. Who has a job to do? Do you hear their thoughts? Do they complain aloud? Where is the poem happening? Is it out of doors, in a January coppice? Is it in a cottage, sun flooding through the open door? On the bend of a muddy track? Who is watching?

Write a first draft. Read it aloud. At this stage, be generous to your new poem and yourself. Feel the excitement of something new and pursue what's pleasing you. You might want to do some extra research, and this can throw up fresh ideas too.

Is the order of the poem in this early draft the best it can be? Poems can arrive quickly, but later you may spot that stanza 3 is stronger if it comes after stanza 4. Perhaps you don't need stanza 4 at all.

Think about the shape and form of your poem. Add white space (or take it away). Read it aloud again. Is every word working? Are there places where your poem loses its rhythms? Adjust. Prune. Read it aloud again for the lovely sounds.

Think hard about the last lines of your poem. Does it stop in the right place? Often, we write on past the place where the poem really stops. We try too hard to explain the meaning, but really, it was there all along.

Enjoy yourself, and may your poetry prosper!

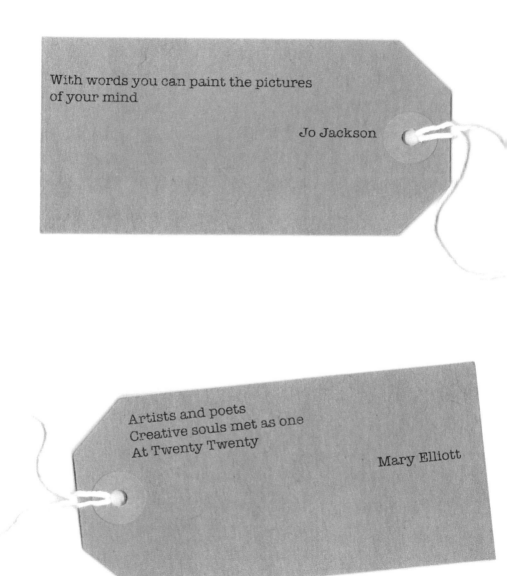

With words you can paint the pictures
of your mind

Jo Jackson

Artists and poets
Creative souls met as one
At Twenty Twenty

Mary Elliott

BEHIND THE SCENES

Machines rely on a variety of cogs and wheels which contribute to their smooth running, and Wenlock Poetry Festivals were no different. A vast array of people, mainly volunteers, ensured that each of them was an enjoyable and uplifting experience for everyone – poets and audiences.

Weeks and months beforehand, contributors had to be contacted, venues and schedules organised and programmes printed. Poets were met at stations and taken to wherever they were staying. New friends were made, nerves soothed, and the end product made all the stress worthwhile.

Most of this activity was invisible and can perhaps be likened to bees in a hive working away to produce honey – the final result of all their hard work. Without all the goings-on behind the scenes, the wonderful Festivals would not have happened. Huge thanks is owed to all those amazing, hardworking folk whose belief in the power of poetry kept them going.

Angela Piddock

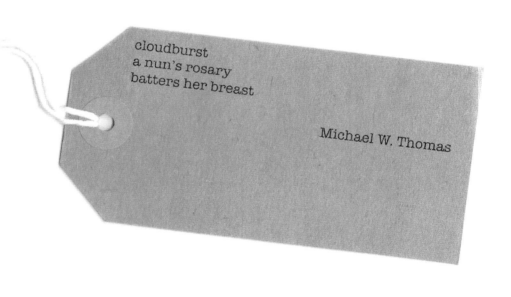

cloudburst
a nun's rosary
batters her breast

Michael W. Thomas

Liz Lefroy

In the Making

Sometimes, like parking a car, making this book's
been an edging in, a checking of angles, edging out

to start from scratch, turn the wheels until they're in kilter,
using the car in front – the one that's perfectly parked –

as a spirit level. Sometimes, in making this book,
I've felt how I imagine the driver of the Toyota felt

this morning. I saw the part when he was revving
too hard, then mounted the pavement, began

floundering. As with parking a car, sometimes the making's
been smooth-going, like the time outside the old house

when I manoeuvred into a slot so tight it seemed
(to the naked eye) smaller than the car itself.

I got in on the first attempt, at ease on account
of my doing this same thing over and over at all hours,

the car ending up no more than a perfect
inch from the kerb, neat as a set of ironed sheets.

Like the driver of the silver Toyota, sometimes
I've felt myself faltering. A memory about parking helps

me to understand about the way I've relied, for this
book and its making, on my friends and my sons,

their flair and assurance. That time, I wedged my Chevette
into a shape that was wrong for her. I was twenty, in flip-flops,

and stuck, so I flapped home, called for my mother.
She came down the street, flour on her wrists, parked like an angel.

Frieda Hughes

Purple Triangles

There are scraps of poems heaped and left
Lying all over the house
That I have no memory of writing:
Scribbles of thoughts, some of which rhyme;
Ideas for much longer poems
Or poems that will make your head spin
With their irrefutable truth:
Poems that might describe you to yourself
Or someone else;
That might have leaked from a hole in the tip
Of one of my fingers, as if it were a tap,
Or dripped from my hair
As I wring it out after washing,
Or been scraped from beneath my fingernails
After planting azaleas among the hellebores.
Their voices rise like coloured shapes
Between these walls of books and paintings;
Green squares, orange ovals, and kites of purple triangles
Clamour in anticipation for emancipation:
Finish me! Finish me!
Make me whole, give me purpose,
Set me free.

R.V. BAILEY

Occupation

Doctor? Not what you think, if you
Think at all. No blood or bandages.
(Something to do with hearts...?)

To mention *Writer* as an alternative,
Suggests celebrity idleness. Yet the form
(There is always a form) requires

Some indication of what I get up to
In the usual working hours. *Poet's*
A questionable title: furtive, even:

A kind of burglary suggests itself.
Decidedly a suspect calling – a
There and not-there sort of thing:

Nothing you'd notice. Maybe even
A body-snatcher (almost respectable, in
Its time), digging up what was perhaps

Better left buried. A picker-up of trifles;
Things left idly lying about. A thief –
Of thoughts, words, hopes, that

Properly belong to others, though it's I
Who overhear them. Quite honestly

I've still no idea what's the right term
To put on the form.

Paul Francis

How to Make a Festival

First, take a Shropshire market town
sprinkled with a variety of trees,
its juices oozing history –
the narrow High Street, Guildhall, Corn Exchange.
More timbered buildings than a visitor
can photograph. Site of Olympian Games.
'The perfect place for poetry'.
Says who? We'll come to that.

You'll need a base. Why not choose Wenlock Books
possessor of the national Golden Nib
for Independent Bookshop of the Year?
Hours of labour, years of love.
There on the wooden stairs, amid displays,
Anna is wondering what might come next:
maybe, a poetry festival?

It isn't her idea. Comes from a friend
who, by coincidence, is Poet Laureate.
Anna's not one to let a chance go by.
"So long as you're the patron." It's a deal.
The 'perfect place' quote comes from Carol Ann.

The mix expands. Now take a clove
of backroom saints, committed, slightly mad.
Stir in the poets, programme, ticket sales;
accommodation, transport, website, grants.

Recruit then organise the volunteers.
A lorryload of books. So much to do.
There's never quite enough of them and
24/7 isn't long enough but
these are believers, and they make it work.

Around the edges of the pan
an altruistic flavour – volunteers
to staff events, the office, Poetree.
Have poets to stay, drive them around,
negotiate a trail with local shops,
pick up the pieces, cover up the cracks.
This is a tiny town but for the cause
there's hordes of helpers. Nearly what they need.

Then finally – to make it simmer right –
you need three days of sunshine.
Not even Amazon can promise that
but for the Wenlock Poetry Festival, somehow
the gods are happy to oblige.

Each spring, for seven years, we get this feast:
big names, discoveries, familiar friends
whisking around this ancient, compact town
and smiling, at the buzzing in our heads,
the words, the phrases, lines.

Poetry flies in
Wenlock Books the catalyst
Love, joy, depth of word

Melanie Revolta

Pat Edwards

On the Edge

Sometimes, even when the poets are reading,
I am removed a moment, lifted out of myself.
Looking on, I see the audience listening hard,
hear them breathe in the messages, like water
running under ice, or light filtered through trees.
And I tell myself, we did this, we made this happen.
My town is mostly unaware, has no idea who these
poets are. We have drawn them here, done good;
have used precious resource, a year in the making,
for this magic to happen. It has held us on the edge,
waiting for funds, waiting for support, waiting for you.
Sometimes, even as the lights go out, doors close,
I am removed a moment, go back to the very start,
know each year we made this, built it with our heart.

Bethany Rivers

Behind the Scenes

From the first glint of the organiser's inspiration for a poetry festival,
the notes, the plans, discussions in committee, obtaining funding,
applications, sponsors, programming, to recruitment of staff and
volunteers, to ascertaining which poets will perform, be interviewed,
the where and the when and the what about and who by, all those
swimming 'w' questions, the why and the how of logistics of transport,
accommodation, venues, to marketing and selling of tickets, and
the raison d'être which drives it all: the deep intent to give the gift
of poetry to many ears who will listen, receive, be moved
or entranced by poets' words and presence, perhaps
for many years after: the results of all the headaches
of worry, the sheets of sweat, the multi-coloured post-it notes,
the endless lists, the frantic phone calls, the lost and re-sent emails,
all the liaising and finalising, until –

that precious droplet of silence
(before the applause), occurring just after
the last syllable of the poem is spoken, that
unique vibration of the crafted words
flowing from the writer's deep attention
to the intertwining of internal landscapes
and external elements: this falls into and becomes
an indelible imprint in the body of the listener,
like the water's memory of a speckled grey pebble
skimming across a lake when the sun glances
at just the right angle, to display diamonds of ripples,
the ones you can never catch,
but must always believe in.

Carol Forrester

Open Mic Mistakes

You've forgotten the microphone,
or forgotten to charge the receiver
to plug into the amp you don't understand
squealing by the stage. Again.

Worse still, is if you forget the amp,
because no number of microphones,
new batteries, or functioning receivers
work without the bastard box.

You've forgotten the introductions,
left them on the printer, the coffee table,
4G has fled the building
so the email backups will not load.

You will have to flub it.
Smile through the stumbling, project
your voice, your confidence
in the hopes it will be enough.

Most of the time it is.
Most of the time you are surrounded
by poets, and poems, and words
which will make everything good.

Beverley Fry

Festival Artist 2011

I leave behind the busy busy and the everyday
as an invitation came my way to guest as artist.
I'd get up, out of bed, leave the chit-chat
and radio four's news   at nine   at one   at ten.
Be an Artist-witness to poetry at Wenlock Festival.
Have a whole weekend lost in words.
A bright new spell from normal life.

In my 2011 art book is a sketch of a poet in a pulpit,
sun pouring in, he almost has a halo.
And look – here's a study of Miriam Margolyes,
not a sound as she reads that year's collection.
Her feet can't reach the ground from the great oak throne.
Another drawing – a sculptor wearing goggles.
He chips words in stone, cuts their spaces,
their reach, the breaths between, beneath, above, below.

We rushed to venues, with so much to hear
and see in two enchanting days. Or was it three?
And always sunny but Easter daffodils had passed.
I noticed petals on our shoes and trampled grasses.

Look and listen. Let my pen express the scene.
My captured mind in gentle hands.
A Poet's hand and heart sets my pen free.
Free to draw, forget that list of jobs never done,
that every day stuff, the chit-chat   and the news at one.

Roger Garfitt

At the Rock Face

i.m. Norman Nicholson

I actually think what we do is harder
than what Shelley and Byron and those people
had to do – wrapped in the thick dressing gown
I had lent you against the cold of my cottage
on Anglesey, half-turned away so that you were
looking into the blank of the television screen
as if it were the silence you had to quarry
on half a lung...
                            And then to see you
'Landing on Staffa', driving a new form like a coach-and-six,
        flexing the long lines against the short,
"the describers" all at work, Scott, Keats, Wordsworth,
        ("each the other's blight,
hurried and hurrying") before you scurried south,
        "down the ragged rip
of the tartan, to grey unphotographed
        waste acres of West
Cumberland. There, in dark claustrophobic
        winter, to retrace
lonnings once known to the feet of childhood".

I was to discover just how fertile those winters were
when you sent 'The Bloody Cranesbill', a recovery
of the weekly walk with your father and your Uncle Jim
across the ruddled rocks of the mine's long dying
to the cockle-shell dip in the limestone where you found
a flower "fragile as Venetian glass, pencilled with metal-
    thread
Haematite-purple veins. The frail cups lay so gently
On their small glazed saucer-bracts that a whisper would have
    tipped them over
Like emptying tea leaves out."
                            How delicate it is,
that first glimpse beyond us, just as you were learning
to read the town back to the iron ore it made its living from.

And it's an awareness you never lost. Alive to all the detail
as "the earth scratches itself awake" and "codlins-and-cream
and comfrey crane up from hairy necks through collars
of bicycle wheels and broken pots", you'd pick your way
through scrap to the whitlow-grass, reclaiming its place
on the foreshore "with a flower no bigger than a
    whitebait's eye."

CLOSING NIGHT

For *Closing Night* read *Climax*. Any Festival builds and grows, producing highlights along the way, but the finish comes with anticipation of extra excitement, something to take home with you and remember. It's a night when the best-known, most glittery stars come to town – the Poet Laureate of England, the National Poet of Wales, Scotland's Makars past and present.

You settle in, happy in the certainty that something special is about to sweep you up in its arms.

Tim Cook

School, shop, green and square.
Poetry lives everywhere.
Wenlock hosts, poets dare.

Melanie Revolta

Jackie Kay

Bandstand

Imagine then on this old bandstand,
in this great park, where the trees
have congregated for years,
all the artists have gathered
firmly here, on the wooden floor,
passionate as peace protestors.

And the brass band plays the songs.
And the poets read *The Storm Cone.*
And the photographers catch the goings-on.
And the artist sees the stark future
roar over the mound of the hill,
down the road towards the open stage,

and somebody shouts *Venceremos!*

Hannah Lowe

Fires

They were lighting fires, my mother and father.
Autumn and they'd stack and prod the pyre
then stand on either side, smoking cigarettes,
the flames between them like a giant gate.
What was it they were burning? I still don't know.
Once I watched them from an upstairs window,
a marble in my mouth – red, gold, copper.
I didn't mean to swallow those fire colours.

At the hospital, they took an X-ray.
We saw it floating in my belly, a grey
flat spore. *It will soon come out*, the doctor
was sure. Now everything is gone forever,
my parents, the ashen garden, the tangled trees
but still that ball of fire spins in me.

Katrina Naomi

Nothing Biblical

No parting
but some days you sense
makes way
a person's need
stretching from here
and beyond
there's a pause between
and their moshing
between the mundanity of chores
swimming is the high point of a day
some mornings it allows
the orange buoys pop back up
loll towards Newlyn
even if other things
your list
the sea
a communication
of empathy

of waves
the sea
as if it understands
the sea having plenty of itself
to the States
Atlanticking
the rollers
between downpours
you suspect
the sea knows this
ease to a swim
damp Belisha beacons
something to aim for
fall from
you've done this
and you
the sea showing what it can
most days it's enough

Ann Gray

My Blue Hen

I sing to my blue hen. I fold her wings
against my body. The fox has had her lover,
stealing through the rough grass,
the washed sky. I tell her, I am the blue heron
the hyacinth macaw. We have
a whispered conversation in French. I tell her
the horse, the ox, the lion, are all in the stars
at different times in our lives. I tell her there are
things even the sea can't do, like come in when
it's going out. I tell her my heart is a kayak
on wild water, a coffin, and a ship in full sail.
I tell her there is no present time,
an entire field of dandelions will give her
a thousand different answers. I tell her
a dog can be a lighthouse, a zebra finch can
dream its song, vibrate its throat while sleeping.
I tell her how the Mayan midwife sings each child
into its own safe song. Tonight, the moon holds back
the dark. I snag my hair on the plum trees. I tell her
I could've been a tree, if you'd held me here long enough.
I stroke her neck. She makes a bubbling sound,
her song of eggs and feathers. I tell her you were
a high note, a summer lightning storm of a man.

Pauline Prior-Pitt

The Dead

They walk with you,
the dead.

Some skip along in front,
some walk beside
some, like naughty children,
drag behind.

Others walk on top of you,
crush you into nothing,
or demand to be carried
like shopping.

A few slip like loose change
into pockets.

And one or two
lie curled together,
stitched into the lining of your heart.

Liz Lochhead

Chimney-Sweepers

Maytime and I'm
on a fool's errand
carrying home this bunch of the dandelion clocks
which Shakespeare called *chimney-sweepers*
and a friend tells me his wee granddaughter
in the here-and-now calls *puffballs*.
I'm holding my breath, and them, this carefully
because I want to take them home and try
to paint them, although
one breath of wind and in no time
I'll be stuck with nothing but a hank of
leggy, limp, milky pee-the-bed stalks
topped with baldy wee green buttons, for
golden lads and girls all must
as chimney-sweepers come to dust.

On daisy hill by the railway bridge
one lone pair of lovers laze in the sun.
A little apart from her, he lounges
smoking a slow cigarette and waits
smiling, half-watching her weave a bluebell chain
that swings intricate from her fingers, hangs heavy
till she loops it, a coronet upon her nut-brown hair.
I'm wondering is this to be her *something blue*?

She calls out to me, I to her,
as folk do in these days of distancing
and I can hardly believe it when she says
she never in all her childhood
told the time by a dandelion clock.

She's up to her oxters in ox-eye daisies, this girl.
The ones my mother, Margaret,
always called *marguerites* but never
without telling me again how my father
writing to her from France before Dunkirk or after D-Day
always began his letters *Dear Marguerite.*

The saying goes that a maiden
crowned by bluebells can never tell a lie
the girl informs me, solemn as she
crosses her fingers, each hand held high,
the smoke from her lover's cigarette
almost but not quite as blue as
the frail blooms – time, truth and a promise – that she
braided together on this their one-and-only
sure-to-be-perfect Summer's day.

Oh *Marguerite   Margaret*   my Mum
who never got to be as old as I am today
did you ever hear tell of this proverb?
Oh Mum how much I wish I could ask you
this and so many other
small and silly things, but
golden lads and girls all must
as chimney-sweepers come to dust.

Pascale Petit

Roebuck

(Poem beginning with a line by Lucie Brock-Broido)

Tell me there is a meadow, afterwards,
that the roebuck will come
to the top of my garden,

that the window will cut me
with glass blades
of dewy hooves.

That I'll lay out my doe mask,
my necklace of icicles,
onto the deep windowsill.

Tell me the buck will be there
among nettles and briar, his mouth
panting, his lungs clear.

That his legs won't tangle
in the electric wire
around my tower.

That if he can't find his way
back into the before,
his horns jewelled

with thorns and flowers
might grow into a tall grove.
Tell me that even in my solitude,

my altar goods laid out
to the god of woods,
that this red buck

against the steep viridian field
will sprout a ladder between his tines
that I can climb.

That his antlers will be strong
as my spine, that I will scale
the rungs of myself

out onto the clouded
chancel of the sky, my body
slick as a newborn fawn.

The Forest asks: what are you Deer?
  And Deer answers –
I am the breeze of the grass as I sprint
I am the bones of the roots
I am the skin of brown tree trunks

Sammy, Year 5

Gillian Clarke

An Egret at Portmeirion

after the conference

Evening silence and the crowds are gone
leaving a quiet hour, two alone
watching a lonely egret on the shore,
recalling all we share, art, life, and more,
designs and dreams, ideas, harmonies,
buildings, beauty, culture, histories.

At the edge of things the sea's retreat,
the come and go of water, salt and sweet,
draws the Dwyryd's tides in waterlight
the way a word, lines drawn on paper might
house us, unite us, Europeans all,
one force against the rise and fall of fools,

who clamour, cackle, crow. They come, they go,
less than an egret's feather on the flow.

CAROL ANN DUFFY

Virgil's Bees

Bless air's gift of sweetness, honey
from the bees, inspired by clover,
marigold, eucalyptus, thyme,
the hundred perfumes of the wind.
Bless the beekeeper

                    who chooses for her hives
a site near water, violet beds, no yew,
no echo. Let the light lilt, leak, green
or gold, pigment for queens,
and joy be inexplicable but *there*
in harmony of willowherb and stream,
of summer heat and breeze,
                         each bee's body
at its brilliant flower, lover-stunned,
strumming on fragrance, smitten.

                         For this,
let gardens grow, where beelines end,
sighing in roses, saffron blooms, buddleia;
where bees pray on their knees, sing, praise
in pear trees, plum trees; bees
are the batteries of orchards, gardens, guard them.

VOTE OF THANKS

Jeff Phelps

Memories of Wenlock Poetry Festival

One of my strongest memories is of walking up Much Wenlock High Street on a Saturday morning of the Festival and coming across Poet Laureate Carol Ann Duffy. She was standing in the market, perfectly engrossed, picking up plants and vegetables and examining them. carefully. I wondered whether she was considering buying or was devising a new poem. Maybe both. It seemed too absurd that the little town was teeming with first-rank, internationally known poets, but that's what happened and it drew in poets and enthusiasts from all over.

I remember reading at an event in Priory Hall and hearing laughter and loud conversation coming from the next room. Afterwards I discovered that Andrew Motion had been holding forth to a table full of friends and fans in the adjoining cafe.

What joyous weekends they were. You could walk up to the Edge Arts Centre and be sure to meet someone you knew on their way there or back to the town. You could sit on the green with your sandwiches and have a conversation with someone you hadn't seen for a year. You could sit late in the courtyard of one of the pubs, making new friends that you'd stay in touch with years later. There was such warmth in the gatherings, whether in the Priory Hall or The Edge, in Wenlock Pottery or any of the other official and unofficial venues – genuine enthusiasm and concentrated listening. We never failed to leave the weekend inspired and refreshed.

Thank you, Anna Dreda, for inventing it, and to all for making it happen.

THE AFTERPARTY

I tell Anna Dreda over and over that the flame from Wenlock Poetry Festival, much like the Olympic torch, has passed to us here in the Poetry Pharmacy – from the Poetry Breakfasts to the events in the garden, the workshops, Anna's poetry book club for children and her reading of "The Night Before Christmas" by candlelight, down to the rug from the bookshop.

We are so grateful to be part of that afterparty of prosecco and the burning bright flame that is poetry.

Deborah Alma

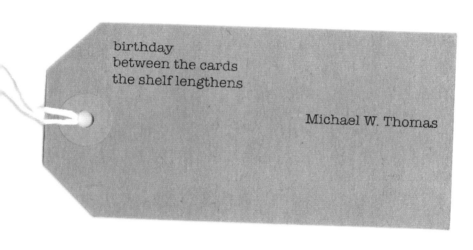

birthday
between the cards
the shelf lengthens

Michael W. Thomas

Long After the Afterparty

It is impossible to unsay the unsayable.
That is, to put all of the words back
in their little boxes
then arrange them into piles
of verbs, adjectives, nouns and so on.

It is furthermore inconceivable
to pick apart a metaphor, dismantle a simile
or take the eyes and hearts from an image
and stopper into jars of formalin
like dead things.

A poem is not a dirty penny
lost in a storm drain.
A poem is not an empty crisp packet
shoved down the back of a sofa.
A poem wants to highwire dance with you.

Once released from the lips,
it funnels into your ears
and lights up the brain's right hemisphere.
It becomes tricky then, to shake its hullabaloo
from the skull's wunderkammer.

Months later, when the chairs
are stacked with dust in a utility room
a poem will grab you and turn on its tunes,
pop a bottle of fizz –
all agency, all whoosh and abracadabra.

STEVE HARRISON

After the Poetry Party

There must have been a poetry party in 2016
as it's far too tidy on Church Green
except for the shred of paper,
a straggle of baler twine: remnant of a Poetree
that's blown into the iron railings around William Brookes' tomb.

Over the Priory Wall, workshop words are washing around the lavabo,
clipped evergreen Wombles watching for littered rhymes.
There are tracks of an ambulance,
parked up for hours, but nobody minds.
Dr D. administers her prescriptives, the nurse does her verse.

A wine glass in The George and Dragon
has lipstick traces of a Poet Laureate as
the dominoes curse the bloke who boxed
their Sunday ritual with poems from Milton Keynes.

In the quarries on Wenlock Edge, there are recent boot marks
newer than the Limestone Cowboys, printed by a posse of poets.
Run your fingers down the bark, like a needle on vinyl,
on the trees on Linden Field: you'll hear the applause
from The Edge Arts Centre, feel the poet's broad smile
beaming around the air in other people's stories.

A chocolate bar wrapper swept under a classroom cupboard
from a Hollie McNish workshop unfolds a dozen future poems.
In the library a resident poet still excavates
The Guardian for his next sonnet.

The bloke from The Bilash boasts at serving
Daljit Nagra a Bangladeshi Naga,
Gregory Leadbetter a Vegetable Paratha.
The Methodist Chapel offered its pulpit and pews
to four-and-twenty Salopians
none of whom have turned out ropey 'uns
and still practise what they preached.

Tea on the Square had Poetry Breakfasts
with rhymes snap, crackle and popping.
The ghosts of Wenlock Books still haunt
the ones who descended to on-line shopping.

Bees live in the tent peg holes of the Busk marquee,
compare the variety of poems at the last wedding –
not a patch on Liz's flipping great flip chart.
They use the hay bale straw as bedding.

From this tiny harbour in the hills
where the poetry surpassed us,
how fitting that this Olympian town
once had its own Parnassus.

Above the blackened
trunk hollowed by rain
sweet chestnuts flourish

Jeff Phelps

WILL MCCARTNEY

Muscle Memory

They say that our muscles have memory –
that our flesh 'n' bone has a flashback zone
where our sinews' subconscious
can re-unlock a step and a strut and a samba,
where our toes remember that two-step trick
which undoes the stubborn stick of the dance floor's grip,
where our lips remember that calculated sip
that combats drips and fuels hips,
where our legs summon up how to stand in line,
how to navigate frantically
to the front left to kick out the alt right
and to swell and surf and predict and interpret
the pulsing heart of the place we're in.

They say that our muscles have memory –
that our paws recall that lilting aerial punch,
that our ears still hold dear the pause
for breath before the conductor's clinical blow,
that our shoulders reminisce how to wriggle and rub
in flawless formation with no-one we know,
that our eyes can look back at those brilliant beacons
that burst through the sweat and blur,
and to the next day's sun, cheekily creeping up on us,
as the citadel's swansong sings us home.

Kate Innes

The Armageddon Afterparty

*Winner of the 'Festival in a Book' Poetry Competition
judged by Helen Ivory and Martin Figura*

After lift-off – it was just a little while
before cocktails were served
in the tungsten gravity glasses
and the passengers could float and mingle
and see through the forward reinforced window
the spaceships of the other trillionaires
glinting in cold sunlight
some less, some more phallic and streamlined
and behind them the trundling cattle trucks
of robotic slaves, ready to work on arrival
at their clean, pneumatic future
No one was looking out the rear window
where a blue sphere smeared with grey smoke
and red dust grew smaller and smaller

They drank more before purging, and more again
It would be a long, long voyage
They would slingshot the moon
then sleep in luxury life-support pods
But for now, the lucky ones could toast
their future, their foresight,
that campaign of universal imperialism
that demanded sacrifice
in experiments without atmosphere
The next planet was perfect – primed
They could knock back another one

Behind them, Earth loosened her belt

lopsided cookhouse:
generations of shoulders
in easy gossip

Michael W. Thomas

The Field asks: what are you Rabbit?
     And Rabbit answers -
I am the nibbler of dandelions
I am the digger of ditches
I am the ruler of dawn and dusk
I am the queen of spring and summer

Esther, Year 5

176

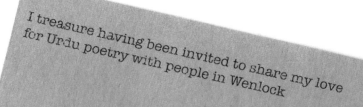

I treasure having been invited to share my love
for Urdu poetry with people in Wenlock

Marion Molteno

Worker bees buzz unheralded
Gathering nectar
Creating conditions places
Hives for Honey poetry

Bare bones embrace. Tree -
reclining, skeleton, hench.
Post-reading nerves ease.

Charlotte Rigarlsford

Acknowledgements

The poems in this anthology which have been published previously are listed below, along with their places of publication. They are reprinted by kind permission of the poets and, where applicable, the publishers.

A Modest Proposal, Philip Gross. *Poetry Ireland Review*, 128, July 2019.
An Egret at Portmeirion, Gillian Clarke. *The Irish Times*, 19th February 2022.
At the Much Wenlock Poetry Festival, Ross Donlon. *Lucidity*, Mark Time Books, 2017.
At the Rock Face, Roger Garfitt. *Comet*, the magazine of the Norman Nicholson Society, September 2022.
Bee Dress, Julia Webb. *Bird Sisters*, Nine Arches Press, 2016.
Blue Heaven, Liz Berry. *Poetry Review*, Winter 2019.
Bluebells, Tess Jolly. *Bad Lilies*, www.badlilies.uk/tess-jolly, 2023.
Border Woman, Jen Hawkins. *Moth*, Mark Time Books, 2023.
Building my Grandfather, Jonathan Edwards. *My Family and Other Superheroes*, Seren, 2014.
Chimney-Sweepers, Liz Lochhead. *A Handsel, New and Collected Poems*, Polygon Books, 2023.
Fires of Sedgley Beacon, Roy McFarlane. An earlier version was commissioned for Dr R.M. Francis Chain Coral Chorus Project.
From here on up all the paths are informal, Jo Bell. *Kith*, Nine Arches Press, 2015.
Geography Lesson, Brian Patten. *Juggling with Gerbils*, Puffin Books, 2000.
Holi, Chrissie Gittins. *A Poem for Every Day of the Year*, edited by Allie Esiri, Macmillan Children's Books, 2017.
Invaders, Morar Lucas. *Retrospective*, Cairn Time Press, 2017.
Jabberwocky, Lewis Carroll: set to music by LiTTLe MACHiNe. Full credits and original link: youtube.com/watch?v=KdlP_6Ooj2E
Judy Dog's Secret, Roger Stevens. *The Waggiest Tails*, Otter-Barry Books, 2018.
Last Night, I Saw the City Breathing, Andrew Fusek Peters. *Mad, Bad and Dangerously Haddock*, Lion Publishing, 2006.
Letter to Professor Walcott, Daljit Nagra. *The Times Literary Supplement*, January 21st 2021.
March, Isobel Dixon. *A Whistling of Birds*, Nine Arches Press, 2023.
My Blue Hen, Ann Gray. *The Moth*, first published as winner of the Ballymaloe International Poetry Prize, 2014.
Occupation, R.V. Bailey. *Yours, etcetera*, Indigo Dreams Publishing, 2019.

our bluest Drop, Mario Petrucci. *afterlove*, Cinnamon Press, 2020.

Peak, Luke Wright. *Peak*, Nasty Little Press, 2023.

Pry'vit, Carole Bromley. Winner of the *Caterpillar Poetry Prize*, 2022.

Purple Triangles, Frieda Hughes. *Alternative Values*, Bloodaxe, 2015.

Roebuck, Pascale Petit. *New Humanist* (Vol. 134, No. 2) and *The Manhatten Review* (Vol. 20, No. 2 Fall/Winter 2022/3).

The Dead, Pauline Prior-Pitt. *Be an Angel, Selected Works*. Longstone Books, 2017.

The Glass Aisle, Paul Henry & Brian Briggs. Full credits and original link: theglassaisle.bandcamp.com, 2018.

The Kindness, Stevie Ronnie. *Bloodaxe: The Poetics of the Archive*, Newcastle University (online, 2015).

The Queue for the Kiss-gate, Paul Henry. *The Spectator*, December 10th 2022.

The Runaway Teeth, Sally Crabree. Illustrator and narrator, Daisy Rickman. Original link vimeo.com/234343352

The Shropshire Carol, Gill McEvoy. written for, and performed by, Polly Bolton's choir *Larks* (Ludlow).

The Washing Machine, Catherine Graham. Winner of The Jo Cox Poetry Prize in memory of Jo Cox MP. *Not in the Plan*, Carers UK, 2017.

The Weathering of Wenlock Priory, Jean Atkin. *How Time is in Fields*, Indigo Dreams Publishing, 2019.

The Well, David Whyte. From *Still Possible*, Many Rivers Press, 2020. Originally published in *Pilgrim*, 2012.

Uncle Billy is Teaching Me How to Whistle, Shauna Darling Robertson. *Saturdays at the Imaginarium*, Troika Books, 2020.

Unpeeled, Alison Brackenbury. *The Spectator,* 2019.

Venus, Goddess, Mother, Deborah Alma. Commissioned by Mid Wales Arts Centre as part of their Poetry and Film Project *Six of the Best*, March 2021.

Virgil's Bees, Carol Ann Duffy. *The Bees*, Picador, 2011.

warm milk, Daniel Sluman. *single window*, Nine Arches Press, 2021.

Washing my mother's hair, Char March. *The Thousand Natural Shocks*, Indigo Dreams Publishing, 2011.

We Are Coming, Kim Moore. *All The Men I Never Married*, Seren, 2021.

Whisht, Gregory Leadbetter. *The Fetch*, Nine Arches Press, 2016.

Woman's Hour, Meg Cox. *A Square of Sunlight*, smith | doorstop, 2021.

Wren, John Foggin. *Much Possessed*, smith | doorstop, 2016.

Y Goeden ellyg, Y Mans, Pontardawe, Menna Elfyn. *Tosturi*, Barddas, 2022.

Index of Poets & Poems

The Poetree

Many thanks to Dawn Allen and Jean Atkin for coordinating the contributions from pupils of Sound Primary School.

Thank you to everyone who helped to make this book. It's been a wonderfully generous collaboration.

Here's to Poetry: past, present, and future!

Liz Lefroy